The People's History

Images of
Seaham

by

Trevor Williamson

Council workmen preparing a roadway on the Deneside Estate, *c.* 1935. On the left is Bobby Ballantyne and on the right Jack Dixon.

Previous page: The author's maternal great-grandmother, Annie Blanche Wicks (née Robinson), captured in a candid pose at the back gate of 51 Doctor's Street, New Seaham, *c.* 1920.

Copyright © Trevor Williamson 1999

First published in 1999 by

The People's History Ltd
Suite 1
Byron House
Seaham Grange Business Park
Seaham
Co. Durham SR7 0PY

ISBN 1 902527 06 2

Contents

A striking aerial shot of St John's Church, Blandford Place, showing memorial stones *in-situ* in the burial ground, *c.* 1954. The picture was taken by Jack Braithwaite, a Leeds-based photographer who worked throughout the north in the 1950s. Rubens' Arcade and the National School at the west end of Church Street are visible in the top left with Sophia and Caroline Streets running south. Marlborough Street cuts across the bottom left.

The churchyard was closed by an order of the Queen in Council dated 13th May 1887. Burials, other than those defined as 'exceptional' in the order, were prohibited thereafter, being directed instead to the new cemetery in Princess Road. In the mid-late 1950s the memorial stones were removed to the perimeter walls and the churchyard transformed into a Garden of Rest when the Urban District Council assumed responsibility for its upkeep. A new public walkway linking Church Street and Emily Street was also created which saw the familiar gates at the entrance finally taken down.

Introduction

As a boy growing up in Seaham in the 1960s I took little notice of the changes taking place around me until a school project sparked the interest in local history I have today. My subject was the Candlish Bottleworks, a once thriving and world-famous glass-making factory that had stood just yards from my home in Stewart Street East. Flattened in 1950, there was nothing much left to see, just a wasteland that for years had been my childhood adventure playground, commonly referred to as 'The Bottley'.

From documents at County Hall to interviews with past employees through maps, town guides and newspaper articles, there was, it seemed, an endless trail of information. Yet only pictures could bring it all to life and so I turned to photographer Walter Oughtred whose studio in North Railway Street became the source of my first old prints. From that moment grew an interest in photography and a special fascination with pictures of the past.

More than twenty years on I have many local images, each of which encapsulates a moment in people's lives. Most have been copied from treasured albums containing a unique mixture of amateur and professional prints illustrating places, events and families from bygone days in the town. Looking back through these albums and hearing the stories that go with them has brought countless hours of pleasure which I hope will continue for many years to come. In this book I present some of my personal favourites and reflect on some of those earlier photographers whose images we are fortunate to share today. Perhaps you will also find a favourite of yours amongst them or discover with surprise that you're included too!

Miners from Seaham Colliery in the late 1920s. On the extreme left is Billy Strong. The tool in the foreground, bottom right, is a dreg or form of braking pin which was thrust between the spokes of a moving tub wheel to slow the tub down or bring it to a halt.

Some of Seaham's Photographers

The earliest known reference to photography in Seaham appears in the 1851 census for Dawdon Township which lists John Weight, a 'photographic artist', living as a visitor in Bath Terrace, Seaham Harbour. Photography was then still in its infancy and only 51 professionals were known throughout the country. Finding one in Seaham at that time is therefore quite remarkable.

Trades directories and advertisements in local newspapers suggest that commercial photography became established in Seaham in 1858 when 'Purvis's photographic portrait rooms' were opened in North Terrace. The exact location of this studio is unknown but it was probably at number 22, the trading address for a succession of professional photographers operating in Seaham from the early 1860s to the early 1880s. The list includes James Elliott, James Short, John Charles and John Lomax.

Robert Brotherton and Sidney Stringfellow followed in the 1900s. Little is known about Brotherton or his work but Stringfellow's prints turn up with regular frequency. He arrived in Seaham Harbour around 1911 and worked from a studio at 19 Church Street which he held until his death in 1926.

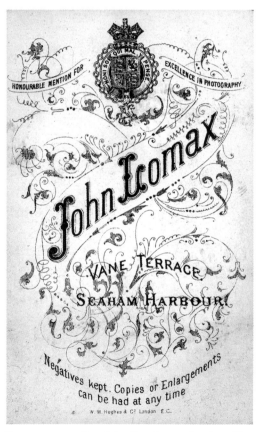

A carte de visite by John Lomax, c. 1880. Lomax practised in Seaham during the late 1870s and early 1880s from numerous studios in North Terrace, Henry Street, Church Street and Vane Terrace. In October 1879 he also took over the Theatre Royal and managed it successfully alongside his photographic interests until 1881 when he finally retired to Rotherham.

Three partners of the Princess Studios enjoying a day out in the Yorkshire Dales, c. 1958. Left to right: Walton Young, Jack Howe and Jim Curry.

Next came Walter Oughtred, Seaham's best known and most prolific commercial photographer. His career spanned 49 years of change in Seaham from 1930 until 1979 when, sadly, he passed away. Meanwhile, around 1954, a new photographic partnership called the 'Princess Studios' started up above Walton Young's chemists shop in Princess Road. Young was one of four partners in the business, the others were Jack Howe, Jim Curry and Walter Bassett. Jack and Jim undertook most of the photographic assignments and have kindly loaned a number of pictures for this book.

Seaham's last professional studio was owned by Jim Greenhalgh who had worked on an ad-hoc basis for the Princess partnership since the early 1960s. In 1969, following the closure of the 'Studios', he went into business on his own at 49 Church Street, continuing until his retirement in 1986.

In addition to this succession of resident professionals there were, of course, many amateur enthusiasts. Amongst the earliest were those led by chemist Robert Forster who sold photographic goods from his shop in Frances Street. Part of the premises were used to host informal gatherings and it was here, on 22nd January 1902, that the town's first amateur association – The Seaham & District Photographic Society – was formed. Disbanded during the First World War it reformed in 1919 and continued until its closure in 1923.

On 25th May 1933, a new amateur club was founded at Rock House Educational Establishment. It too was suspended at the outbreak of war but came together again in the late 1940s and went on to earn widespread acclaim. The club's loyal following still meet in Rock House today.

Photographs taken by these amateurs and professionals are now important visual records of Seaham's past. They paint a unique portrait of bygone days and what follows is a small but fascinating selection.

Acknowledgements

Whilst compiling this book I have had the pleasure of meeting many friendly and helpful people. I would like to convey my appreciation to all and pay special thanks to those who loaned photographs or assisted with the manuscript, in particular:

Les Alexander, Freda Allen, Raymond Armbrister, Lavinia Barstead, Billy Black, Marie Bradley, Ray Brammer, Albert & Mary Brown, Gordon Brown, Pat Bruce, Billy Brunning, Graeme Byers, Alan & Bill Campbell, Doris Chapman, Billy Clifford, Maurice Clyde, Malcolm Critch, Jim Curry, Raymond & Cerise Dalton, Marjorie Defty, John Dinsdale, Joyce & Roland Duffell, Fred & Alice Gillum, Melbourne Green, Bill Griffiths, Joe Guy, Louvain Harman, Johnny Harris, Elizabeth Henderson, Joyce Henry, Chris & Nora High, Les & Olive Hood, Jack Howe, Don Hutchinson, May Islip, Brian Jones, Tom Kelly, Alan Kennedy, Alfred Knapp, Jim Lamb, Arthur & Betty Lanes, Margaret Larder, Godfrey Little, Sylvia Lowery, Chris Miller, Sana Miller, Mary Mortensen, George Nairn, Alan Napier, Vic Oates, Anne Oglesby, Fred & Janet Parrington, Warren Phillips, Ada Pickering, Alan Place, Bobby Pyeburn, Douglas & Isa Rennoldson, Frederick Richardson, Ronnie Robinson, Derek & George Rochester, Dennis & Jacqueline Rooney, Brenda Ross, Miriam & Robbie Rousell, Eric Sheevles, Dave Smith, Neville Stead, Jean Stephenson, Eleanor Stewart, Gladys Stokoe, Rennie Swann, Billy Taylor, Jean Taylor, Freda Tinnion, Ella Totten, Cecil Trotter, Jennie Tulip, Jimmy Turnbull, Betty Weightman, Arthur Wicks, Billy Wicks, Joe & Doreen Wicks, Leonard Wicks, Greta Wilkinson, George Willis, Ernie Wright.

I am indebted to Seaham Park Bowls Club, Seaham Harbour Cricket Club, Dawdon Miners' Social Club, Westlea School, North East Press, Durham Record Office and Sunderland Museum, for permission to reproduce material from their collections and to the staff of Seaham, Durham and Sunderland City Libraries for their friendly and continuing help. I am also grateful to Andrew Clark of The People's History for his patience and encouragement and to David Hutchinson, Colin Johnson and NPS Visual Communications for their help with the photography.

To my immediate and extended family, whose help has been invaluable in the course of recent months, I offer sincere thanks, especially to my parents John and Nancy, who have fortunately emerged unscathed from the storm of merciless questioning. Finally, deepest thanks go to my wife, Glynis and sons Craig and Lewis for suffering from the sidelines for longer than I dare to think. Now the book is published you can breathe a sigh of relief ... until the next one!

SECTION ONE

PEOPLE AND PLACES

Looking down Castlereagh Road past the Drill Hall and Co-operative store, *c.* 1900. The Drill Hall was built at a cost of £4,500 for the 2nd Durham (Seaham) Volunteer Artillery Brigade and was opened by the Marchioness of Londonderry on 27th October 1888. Access to the armoury and men's quarters was via the south entrance shown here in Castlereagh Road, whilst access to the officers' quarters was the via the north entrance in Tempest Place. The castelated wall in the foreground enclosed a large drill and repository ground. Used from 1958 as a cutting room by Barran's clothing manufacturers, it was gutted by fire on 1st March 1986 and demolished a few weeks later.

Schoolchildren from Durham City assembled with teachers and guests during a summer fete at Seaham Hall, 31st August 1911. The event, which marked Lord Londonderry's appointment as Mayor of Durham, was attended by 2,744 children, 108 teachers and 46 members of the Corporation and Education Committee. At the end of the day the huge party gathered in front of the Hall where the National Anthem was sung and photographs were taken. Before leaving, each child received a medal commemorating the event.

Seaham Hall was built by Ralph and Judith Milbanke in 1791-2 on the site of Seaham House, a former medieval manor. The upstairs design included a commodious drawing room which later became famous as the place where their daughter, Anne Isabella, married the poet George Gordon Byron, 6th Lord Byron of Rochdale, on 2nd January 1815.

In 1821 the Seaham estate was purchased by the Londonderry family who considerably enlarged the Hall, one of the biggest undertakings being the construction of a new northern wing, containing kitchens and servants' apartments in 1862. By this time the family had acquired most of the freehold properties in the vicinity, demolishing structures in the process to create an extensive private park around the Hall. In 1861 the Village Green itself was also consumed when the old carriage road from Seaton, which passed through the Green in front of the Hall, was re-routed a few hundred yards to the north.

In June 1915 the Hall was placed at the disposal of the military for use as a War Hospital. Furnished with 112 beds, it treated 3,534 patients during the course of the conflict and was handed back on 31st March 1919. The Londonderry's left in 1922 and five years later gifted the premises to the County Council who spent £20,000 converting it into a tuberculosis sanatorium for women and children. Equipped with 80 beds, it was opened on 25th February 1928 by County Councillor Hedley Mason in the presence of its benefactor, the 7th Marquess.

Seaham Hall Hospital in the 1950s. In 1931 a new west wing was added as part of a £30,000 investment scheme which brought 52 more beds, a welcome operating theatre and a staff annexe to the east, with quarters for the medical officer, matron and 26 bedrooms for nurses and domestics. On 5th July 1948 the Hospital Board assumed responsibility for its management and developed further its role as a cardiothoracic treatment centre.

Right: Patients at Seaham Hall Hospital, 1963. Despite local protests the hospital closed in 1978 and afterwards was sold for use as a hotel. However, the venture proved unsuccessful and in 1988 it was converted into a private nursing home which itself went into liquidation in 1995. Two years later the property was bought by enterprising businessman Tom Maxfield who is currently engaged in a £5 million project to convert the Hall into a world-class hotel. An exciting new chapter in the history of Seaham Hall is now beginning to unfold.

North Road heading north, *c.* 1927. Centre left is the Masonic Hall, erected at a cost of £900 by Parkin Thornton to the design of William Forster, architect and agent to the Marquess of Londonderry. To commemorate the opening a grand ball was held on 6th January 1874, thirty two couples dancing into the early hours to the music of Wetherell's band.

North Road heading south, *c.* 1937. In the bottom left corner a little girl poses for the photographer next to the decorative chains which once graced the old promenade. In the distance are the Londonderry Offices and Terrace Green enclosed by wrought iron railings which, like the chains, were removed to provide metal in the forthcoming war.

Featherbed Rocks and beach railway, *c.* 1907. The railway was used to transport sand and gravel to the block-yard during the enlargement of the docks in 1899-1905. Daring children would walk its length at high tide in a perilous stunt which occasionally ended in tragedy. The last occurred on 11th July 1933 when nine-year-old William Fisher lost his balance, fell into the water and was drowned. Shortly afterwards the railway was dismantled.

The Featherbed Rocks, 1934. For generations the Featherbed Rocks have stood as Seaham's most familiar coastal landmark but today they are barely more than a stump. This picture shows them as they are fondly remembered, their scale indicated by a group of four ladies seated centre left. The spot has been the scene of several tragedies, the most infamous being the brutal murder of eight-year-old Caroline Winter in August 1889.

Construction of the sea wall and promenade, 6th July 1953. In 1948 plans were submitted to the Government to construct a promenade and sea defences necessary to protect the crumbling cliffs along North Road. After prolonged negotiations the project was sanctioned. The first phase of work, to build the sea wall and promenade, began in 1953 and was followed by the addition of 11 groynes in 1955. Total cost was £247,960.

Right: A lorry being extracted from the promenade in the early 1960s. In the late 1950s a succession of storms and heavy seas undermined the sea wall causing the promenade to collapse in several places. Work to repair and upgrade the sea defences was carried out and during the course of the work a lorry delivering concrete to a repair site at the southern end of the promenade fell through a weakened section of the walkway. After a short but embarrassing delay the temporary artistic sculpture was removed. The promenade was re-opened in December 1962.

The Baths, North Road, *c.* 1930. Built in 1834 and demolished a century later, the baths stood on the northern side of the cliffs overlooking 'Bessie's Hole'. In 1861 the Seaham Harbour Marine Hotel Co Ltd was formed announcing its intention to build a hotel on the site, incorporating the Baths as outbuildings. Unfortunately, the capital required, some £3,000, could not be raised and the hotel never materialised.

The Infirmary, Tempest Place, 1968. The Infirmary was built in 1844 by Frances Anne, Marchioness of Londonderry and afterwards was maintained by a levy on ships entering the Harbour. In the First World War it served as a General Hospital for the 4th Battalion DLI, treating some 1,408 wartime patients. Between 1920-64 it was used as the Council Offices but then stood empty until 1969 when, regrettably, it was demolished.

Bath Terrace, *c.* 1903. The ornate building at the end of the terrace is the bank of Messrs Woods & Co which was rebuilt in 1895 on the site of the original premises. Later, it was taken over by Barclays and ultimately sold into private ownership when the new North Terrace branch opened near the entrance to the Docks in 1984.

North Terrace, 1908, showing the Londonderry Offices (right) in their original form. Built in 1857, additional wings were added in 1909 to cater for the increase in administrative activity arising from expansion of the Docks and the sinking of the new colliery at Dawdon. The offices were occupied by Seaham Dock Company until 1965 and have since served as the town's sub-divisional police station.

LONDONDERRY OFFICES, SEAHAM.   10742

A closer view of the Londonderry Offices taken in the 1930s. A tragic accident occurred in the courtyard of the offices on 24th August 1883 when a seaman named George Vine fell whilst carrying out repairs at the top of the flagstaff. He sustained serious injuries and died at the Infirmary a few days later. The inquest, held on 4th September in the Rose and Crown, returned a verdict of 'Accidental Death'.

Right: The statue of Charles Stewart Vane Tempest Stewart, 6th Marquess of Londonderry, in transit at the wagon shops, 1922. Modelled in bronze, it depicts the late Marquess in his garter robes holding drawings of Dawdon Colliery and was the work of John Tweed, whose commissions included the Alfred Stevens monument to the Duke of Wellington in St Paul's Cathedral. Its ultimate destination was the Londonderry Offices where it was erected on a stone pedestal and unveiled by his son, the 7th Marquess, on 19th August 1922.

Looking up Church Street in 1914. In the nineteenth century Church Street was largely a residential area where pilots and tradesmen employed at the Harbour could be found. Most of the retailing businesses were clustered around North Terrace and North Railway Street but, as trade expanded, shops opened up in Church Street and ultimately it developed into the town's main shopping area.

A postcard by R. Johnston & Son of Gateshead featuring a crowded North Railway Street, 1914. From the early 1900s until around the Second World War, Johnston's published a large selection of postcards showing everyday scenes in Durham and Northumberland. Sold under the identity of 'The Monarch Series', the cards were made from high quality photographic images which today are highly collectable, this one costing £25!

Two in a series of pictures taken by Walter Oughtred in the early 1930s showing children outside 14 Green Street (above) and 3 Gunn's Buildings (below). The photographs were commissioned by the Urban District Council as part of the slum clearance and improvement orders issued against properties in Seaham Harbour.

Seaham Harbour (Londonderry) Railway Station and Station Hotel in the 1960s. The station was built in 1886 to replace the original one which had stood since 1855. It was opened to the public without any formal ceremony, the first passengers to pass through the new entrance being those for the 10.45 train for Sunderland on 28th December 1886. During the Second World War it was closed and never re-opened, and after falling into ruin it was demolished together with the Station Hotel in August 1971.

'Sir Hugo' off the rails near Seaham Colliery Station, 19th May 1930. The train carrying 300 passengers was *en route* from Liverpool to Newcastle when, at 4 am, it collided with a stray horse. Fortunately, no-one was injured, although the horse was killed and the front two wheels of the engine bogie were de-railed. Normal service was resumed at 9.00 am.

A postcard from 1903 showing the railway lines once used to transport coal from Seaham Colliery. On the left, heading east towards the Docks, is the former rope-worked incline, the rails of which were taken up in January 1988. Part of the route has since been redeveloped for use by pedestrians and cyclists. On the right is the branch line which connected the colliery with the main coast line.

A classic shot by railway photographer Neville Stead showing a south-bound train passing over Hall Dene crossing in the 1950s. To the right is the former Seaham Hall Station, built in 1875 for private use by the Londonderry family and guests visiting nearby Seaham Hall. It was ultimately sold and converted into a private dwelling. The current occupants, Mr and Mrs Brown, have lived there since December 1992.

Gallery Row, *c.* 1951. Like nearby Fenwick Row, Gallery Row was built in the mid-nineteenth century to cater for employees of the bottleworks. Erected at the southern perimeter of the works, it overlooked the packing yard and eighth 'house' (see page 89). The site was cleared around 1960 and in 1969 was sold to local businessman, Derek Mercer, who started-up a scrap metals business there. It closed in April 1999 and is now awaiting redevelopment.

The Green Drive suspension bridge leading to Dawdon Colliery Recreation Ground, *c.* 1930. Erected out of the Welfare Fund at a cost of over £3,000, the bridge was constructed in steel with wooden decking and spanned a total distance of 365 feet. It was opened by Councillor Joseph Dawson on New Year's Day 1927 and remained in use until 1959 when it was replaced by a tarmac roadway and eventually dismantled in the late 1960s.

David High surrounded by his children in the back yard of 32 Stavordale Street, Dawdon, 1922. David and eldest son James (with black faces) were on their way home after a shift at Dawdon Colliery when they encountered a street photographer who took this treasured family photograph. Standing at the left is David junior and on his father's knee is youngest son Joseph (who unfortunately moved when the photograph was taken). Beside them is Robert and Ada. Eldest sister Margaret is holding Elizabeth at the rear.

Blooms on display in Dawdon Working Men's Club during a chrysanthemum show, sometime in the late 1940s. Held annually in November when 'late' varieties were at their best, the show was fiercely competitive, drawing entries and spectators from all over the district. Standing far right, wearing a cap, is Bill Campbell senior, one of the respected 'big chrysanth men' with son, Bill junior, immediately to his right.

Princess Road, *c.* 1930. On the right is Dawdon Co-op and opposite is Dawdon Working Men's Club with the Princess Theatre next door. In the foreground, left, at number 68, is the butchers shop of Shotton Thubron Hudspith which, like many of the shops in Princess Road, eventually became a private residence. The shop on the opposite corner, at the junction with Rainton Street, still exists today as a newsagents and general dealers.

Birkbeck Villa, *c*. 1886. Erected at New Seaham on the main thoroughfare between Christ Church and Hall Street, the Villa was built as a combined dwelling house and Post Office to the designs of Mr Forster (junior) of Seaham Harbour. It opened for business on Monday 18th October 1886 and was named 'Birkbeck Villa' after the owner, Joseph Birkbeck, who is shown standing with his family at the front of the building.

Mr Birkbeck was appointed postmaster at New Seaham in January 1881 following the death of the late postmaster, William Young. Mr Young had been postmaster since 1867, succeeding Robert Kirby at the former Post Office in Post Office Street which stood opposite New Seaham Vicarage at the entrance to Seaham Colliery. This, New Seaham's first Post Office, was opened on Monday 7th February 1859, John Emmerson being appointed postmaster on the recommendation of Frances Anne, Marchioness of Londonderry.

Mr Birkbeck retired in September 1909 after serving as postmaster for almost 30 years. He was succeeded by Frederick Vasey who transferred the business to his own premises nearby. Meanwhile, around 1900, a sub-office had been established in Stockton Road at the High Colliery, under sub-postmaster Michael Brown. Both are still trading today. Vasey's is now run by Ray and Margaret Wyness, whilst Brown's (better known as Brannigan's after long standing former occupants) has recently been taken over by Barry and Wendy Giles. A succession of residents have lived at Birkbeck Villa since the death of Joseph Birkbeck and today the house is again being offered for sale.

A building gang photographed during the construction of Coronation Buildings, New Seaham, 1902. The elderly gent sitting in the centre with the white beard is George Carr, who erected the houses on land leased from Lord Londonderry. A fore-overman at Seaham Colliery for 27 years, Mr Carr retired in March 1902 but unfortunately died less than two years later, on 21st October 1903.

Butchers Street, 1954. Butchers Street stood in the shadow of the High Pit at Seaham Colliery, overlooking what is now Seaham Town Park. One of the houses was home to Thomas Burt, a hewer at Seaham Colliery and Miners' Lodge Official who gave evidence at the inquest into the 1880 explosion. His cousin, also named Thomas Burt, led the Northumberland Miners and was a former Morpeth MP.

Looking towards the Mill Inn from near the entrance to Seaham Colliery, *c.* 1928. An unusual spectacle was witnessed outside the Inn on 12th December 1905 when a motor car owned by Mr J.E. Murray of Azalea Terrace North, Sunderland, broke down and suddenly caught fire, scattering a crowd that had gathered to investigate. The vehicle, a large and handsome white Darracq, valued at £600, was totally destroyed.

Tenants of the hostel for single aged miners, East View, New Seaham, with resident caretakers Richard & Barbara Bleasdale (standing right and left), *c.* 1937. Commissioned by the Durham Aged Mineworkers' Homes Association, the hostel catered for eight former miners and was built by Messrs T.& E. Curry, using land and bricks donated by Lord Londonderry. Total cost, including furnishings, was £2,800. It was opened on 19th January 1929.

An interesting view of the back of Infants' Street, *c.* 1954. One of New Seaham's lesser known streets, Infants' Street was a small row of cottages which stood at the bottom of California Street, immediately south of the Rainton and Seaham railway line.

Harry (Diddler) Allen and son Ronnie at the back gate of 55 Doctor's Street, New Seaham, *c.* 1933. Harry married Margaret Wicks, the eldest daughter of Walter and Annie Wicks who lived a few doors away at number 51. In addition to Margaret, the family had seven other children – John Henry, Arthur, Louisa, William, Leonard and Walter junior, a midget known widely throughout the town.

The Wicks family in the garden of 51 Doctor's Street, *c.* 1919. Most of the garden was used to grow vegetables but at the bottom, near the fields, pigs and chickens were also reared. The animals were fed on farm or kitchen scraps and a home-made feed called 'crowdie' containing powdered stale bread mixed with coarsely mashed vegetable peelings. In the winter months it was spiced up with oil and a dash of mustard!

Looking towards the top of Deneside from the bottom of Evesham Road, 1950. On the right are the old miners' rows. In the foreground is California Street with Doctor's Street behind. Further up is Mount Pleasant, originally a short row of 20 houses, which in 1886 was extended to the top of the bank. Behind is Viceroy Street which was built at the same time. All were demolished in the late 1940s and early 1950s to make way for the Westlea Estate.

Children at play in the garden of 50 Jasper Avenue, Deneside, 1949. Left to right: Edith Shafto, Annie Wicks (the author's mother), Margaret Mason, Margaret Shafto, Eleanor Shafto and Arthur Wicks.

The author's father, John Williamson, standing beside elder sister Rebecca in the doorway of 124 Bethune Avenue, Deneside, 1937. Both were born at 26 William Street, Seaham Harbour, but moved to Deneside in December 1935 together with two-week-old brother, Thomas, when the family were allocated a council house in Bethune Avenue. Their former home in William Street was ultimately demolished during the slum clearance programme to make way for the housing that now forms Hawthorn Square.

SCHOOLDAYS

A classroom scene at Low Colliery School, New Seaham, *c.* 1911. The school was built in 1857 in the middle of Vane Terrace, part of which still stands today, below the Kestrel pub in Station Road. Structural defects forced its sudden closure on 10th June 1979 and in 1981 it was demolished. Today the site is occupied by factory units forming the Kingfisher Industrial Estate.

New Seaham Boys FC, 1907-8. The photograph was taken three years after the foundation of the Seaham and District Junior League and is contemporary with the beginning of the Bethune Challenge Cup for Seaham and District schoolboys. The cup was donated by the Bethune family in December 1907 in honour of Revd Angus Bethune, Seaham's oldest and longest serving vicar.

Girls from St John's Church of England (National) Schools, c. 1915. Back row, left to right: unknown, Ada Crosby, Annie Lewis, unknown, unknown, unknown, Lizzie Campion. Third row: Ada Roberts, unknown, unknown, Gladys Bowron, ? Davis, Mary Barkess, Winnie Nicholson. Second row: unknown, unknown, unknown, Maggie Dixon, Olive Young, Lena Lawrence, Emma Softley. Front row: unknown, unknown, ? Barkess, Hilda Nelson, unknown, Doris Heckles.

Teachers from St John's Church of England (National) Schools, *c.* 1919. Sitting proudly in the centre is headmaster Richard Bainbridge, whilst at the back, standing immediately left of the drainpipe is Theodore Witham, who later became headmaster of Camden Square Intermediate School.

Infants, class E, Dawdon Council Schools, 1922. Seated third right, second row from the front is Ella Balmer. The schools were opened on 11th August 1910 to serve the community at Dawdon which was expanding rapidly around the new colliery. Facilities were provided for 900 pupils in three separate departments, boys, girls and infants. In 1979 the schools were closed and partially demolished following the transfer of infants to Camden Square and juniors to Princess Road.

Group I infants, High Colliery Schools, New Seaham, 1922. The children seem rather absorbed if not concerned by the actions of the photographer. A diminutive Leonard Wicks, one of the author's maternal great-uncles, is shown second right, third row from the front, sporting the family's distinctive hairstyle.

Tradesmen engaged in the construction of Station Road Intermediate School, *c.* 1930. Designed to accommodate 440 boys and 440 girls, the school was completed at a cost £17,800. It was opened by Alderman James Hoy on 21st June 1930 and was the third new school to be unveiled in less than a fortnight, following Princess Road Secondary (Grammar) School for Girls (11th June) and Camden Square Intermediate (18th June). Councillor F. Young was appointed first headmaster and Miss G. Lawther first headmistress.

Budding chemists at work in the science laboratory at Station Road Intermediate, *c.* 1930. Two boys at the front are weighing a ceramic crucible in what appears to be an exercise in inorganic analysis. On the bench behind another pair huddle dangerously close to the three essential components of any classroom experiment – bunsen burner, tripod and asbestos mat.

Class 2A, Seaham Girls' Secondary (Grammar) School, 1930. Back row, left to right: Anna Blackmore, Joyce Pratt, Doris Greener, Lillian Walton, Nancy Marshall, Irene Dixon, Greta Keeley, Peggy Dunn, Doris Tiffany, Ruby Gilchrist, Edna Greenfield. Middle row: Helen Spoors, Edith Rothwell, Ila Moreland, Mary Potter, Irene Pearce, Mary Cockburn, Norma Creaser, Mary Winlow, Mary Nunn, Elizabeth Marks, Marjorie Aitken. Front row: Cora Mason, Jessie Dalton, Irene Barrett, Ada Pow, Miss Howell (geography teacher), Miss Aird (headmistress), Irene Burnip, Dorothy Laws, Mary Thompson and Beatrice Drown.

Thirteen-year-old Bill Campbell (left) in action for Camden Square boys during the final of the (John) Cochrane Cup, 29th April 1938. After beating Murton 1-0 in the semi-final, the team went on to defeat Silksworth 3-2 in a nailbiting final at Roker Park. They also carried off the Sunderland and District Inter-League Championship and became the only Seaham team to win both competitions in a single season.

Left: A school portrait taken in May 1937 to commemorate the Coronation of King George VI. The scholar is 10-year-old George Carr Rochester, a pupil at Byron Terrace Schools. On the eve of the Coronation, nearly 8,000 children throughout the Urban District received mugs and chocolate from the Coronation Committee. Coronation day proper was, of course, a public holiday which meant a welcome break from studies for teachers and pupils alike.

Girls from Station Road Intermediate School, *c.* 1948. Back row, left to right: Jean Patrick, Mary Bray, Serena Johnson. Second row: Violet Downs, Sylvia Blaney, Maureen Gilchrist, Joyce Waters, Catherine Ainsley, Annie Wicks, Pat Gippert, Ella Brown. Third row: Joyce Savage, Jean Harrison, Ella Shafto, Pauline Davison, Mavis Laverick, Joyce Whitelock, Maureen Mason, Mary Redden, Margaret MacIntosh, Nelly Auluman, Betty Clark, Moira Whitehead. Front row: Shirley Holness, Sheila Curry, Georgina Ritchie, Audrey Pettifer, Elsie Brennan, Margaret Kennedy, Norah Brown, Elsie & Edith Cardy (twins).

St John's Church of England (National) Schools football team, 1950-51. Back row, left to right: Stan Oglesby (teacher), Robert Watson, Robert Coombe, Ronnie Edwards, Keith Bell, Tom Scott, (headmaster). Middle row: Barry Hepple, John Heaton, Arthur Proctor, Ralph Osmond, Graham Harrison. Front row: Keith Wilson, Maurice Clyde.

St Joseph's RC Secondary School football team, champions of the District Catholic Schools League, 1950-51. Standing, left to right: Joe Guy, Alfie Evans, Brian Smith, Billy McCabe, Joe Lennox, Matthew Carr. Seated: James Burns (headmaster), Mick Fury, Alfie Guy, Bob Parker, Frank Hardy, Walter Howarth, Joe Kelly (mathematics & sports teacher).

Children enjoying their Christmas party at High Colliery Schools, 1961. The schools closed in 1968 and part of the buildings was retained for use as a community centre. Today the premises are still standing, though somewhat overshadowed by a neighbouring new medical centre.

St Mary's RC Mixed & Infants Schools, Vane Terrace, *c.* 1964. Built at the south end of the old Chapel and Presbytery, the schools were designed for 310 pupils and cost £1,193 to complete. They were opened on 24th September 1888 but closed in 1969 when teaching was relocated

to the former St Joseph's premises in Station Road. Another relocation followed in 1984 when the present school in Dene House Road was opened.

Christmas celebrations in full swing at Ropery Walk Junior and Infants School, *c.* 1964. Leading the proceedings is headmistress Miss Dorothy Chambers (later Mrs McClurgh), accompanied at the piano by Mrs Elizabeth (Cissy) McCutcheon, widow of John McCutcheon, the late librarian and Council chairman. Mingling with her pupils in the distance is Mrs Joan Raine – calm, collected and almost in control!

Seaham Girls Grammar School 1st hockey team, 1963-64 season. The photograph was taken in 1964, not long before teaching was transferred to the newly built Grammar Technical School at Northlea. Sitting in the centre is captain Jean Braddock who went on to play at County level for Cambridgeshire and whom today, as a coach and umpire, is still actively involved in the game.

Special Policeman George Henderson teaching cycling proficiency in the playground at Ropery Walk School, c. 1966. Behind are the outdoor toilets which disappeared when the old school buildings were demolished in the 1970s. During demolition, former teacher Beatrice Wilson rescued numerous artefacts from the rubble, including the foundation stone of the infants school dating from 1894. It now stands in the entrance of the new school nearby.

THE COLLIERIES

Overmen at Dawdon Colliery, *c.* 1953. On the left is Wally Johnson and on the right, widely known townsman Jack Scratcher. Jack was an active first aider, serving with the Dawdon Colliery division of the St John Ambulance Brigade and a keen runner, competing in his youth at local level as a member of Sunderland Harriers.

Seaham Colliery Low Pit, 1912. The Colliery comprised two shafts, commonly referred to as the Low Pit (downcast) and High Pit (upcast). The Low Pit shaft was divided by bratticing into two portions which were called No 1 Pit and No 2 Pit, whilst the High Pit was also known as No 3 Pit.

Originally, the shafts were owned and worked independently, the High Pit by the Hetton Coal Company and the Low Pit by the Marquess of Londonderry. Sinking began first at the High Pit, then known as Seaton Colliery, on 12th August 1845. Sinking at the Low Pit, known as Old Seaham Colliery, began on 13th April 1849, the first coals being drawn on 27th March 1852. Both pits were amalgamated in November 1864 following the introduction of legislation requiring mines to be equipped with two shafts. Shortly after, the shafts were connected underground by a communicating drift.

Thereafter called Seaham Colliery, the pit was known more commonly as 'The Nack', a name given, some say, by the 'nicky nack' sound once made by the High Pit pulley wheels or by the gears of the corn mill at the foot of the nearby Mill Inn bank. Others claim it was linked to the Mill Inn itself where an unusual collection of 'nick nacks' were permanently on display. Buried amidst the folklore lies the definitive explanation, but faded now from memory it is unlikely to be revealed.

In Memory of

SEAHAM COLLIERY EXPLOSION,

WHICH OCCURRED ON THE 8TH, DAY OF SEPTEMBER, 1880;

When 170 Men and Boys were called from Time into Eternity.

We hope they are in heaven.

When they left their homes at night,
How little did they know
That they should never more return
To their lovely cots below.

Death was nigh, and they knew not
How sudden it would come :
Their souls expired upon the spot,
And left their earthly home.

GOD bless the widows who are left ;
The orphan children too :
Weep not but trust in JESUS,
And he will bring you through.

A memorial card commemorating the catastrophic explosion which ripped through Seaham Colliery at 2.20 am on Wednesday 8th September 1880. The card suggests that 170 lives were lost, although the official number was 164, ranging in age from 14 to 71. Some 181 pit ponies also perished. The disaster is the central subject of the book *Troubled Seams* by John Elliott McCutcheon which was first published in 1955.

Right: Thomas Alexander, *c*. 1878. Born in Ryhope in 1844, Thomas was the only child of Robert and May Alexander and like most of his contemporaries he was destined to a life in the mines. On leaving school he started work as a trapper boy at Seaham Colliery, progressing to hewer to deputy before, sadly, losing his life in the 1880 explosion. On that day he worked beyond the end of his normal shift, standing in for the relieving deputy who didn't report for duty. Tragically, a few hours later he was dead, leaving behind a wife, and four children – Jane, Mary-Anne, Robert and little Jack, only six months old. His name heads the list of victims inscribed on the memorial stone in the garden of remembrance at Christ Church, New Seaham.

Miners ready to go underground at Seaham Colliery in the 1920s. Far right is
Anthony Simpson who lived just outside the entrance to the colliery at No 3
Church Street. Like other miners' rows in the vicinity, Church Street was
demolished around 1960. Its site was grassed over and remained undeveloped
until shortly after the colliery closed when it was sold off in plots for private
housing under the new identity of Christchurch Court.

Members of Seaham Colliery Lodge on the racecourse at Durham during the
1925 Miners' Gala. The coal industry was in deep depression at the time,
prompting a succession of stirring political speeches. Miss Margaret Bondfield
made history as the first woman to speak publicly at the event. Also on the
platform for the first time were the ex-Attorney General, Sir Patrick Hastings
and the former Minister for Mines, Emanuel Shinwell.

Pit ponies at Seaham Colliery stables, 1927. In 1871 the Marquess of Londonderry purchased an extensive estate in Lerwick, Scotland, to breed and rear Shetland ponies for use in the Londonderry Collieries. Surplus stock was auctioned annually in September by Mr Robert Brydon, chief land agent to the Marquess, at his farm in Dalton-le-Dale. The last sale took place in 1899 when the Shetland stud was dispersed.

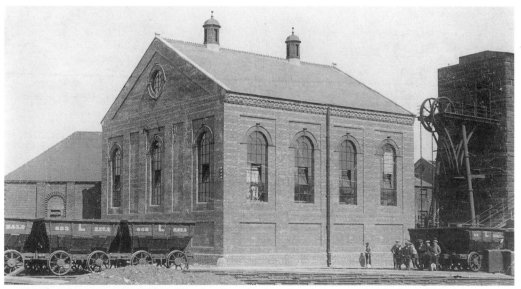

A view of uncertain date, taken during reconstruction of the winding gear at Seaham Colliery High Pit. On the right is part of the original vertical winding engine house and in the centre its newly built successor, awaiting installation of a new conical drum steam winder. The work was carried out several years before an electric winder was introduced at the Low Pit in 1935 and the distinctive twin-engine houses there were dismantled. Electrification of the High Pit followed in 1959.

Workmen at the Londonderry coal depot, *c.* 1934. Crouching in the centre is John Dinsdale with mate Bob Hughes standing right. Behind is an early coal wagon or 'bunker' dating from about 1922.

Workmen in the timber yard at Seaham Colliery about to despatch new skeets for the Low Pit (No 1) shaft, 1947. From the left are: John Williamson, Ernie Rowell, Harry Mortensen, Brian Corkhill, Val Mortensen and Jack Hays. Holding the reigns and just creeping into view is driver, Ned Gray.

Tommy Ridley receiving a retirement gift from Tommy Nicholson in the blacksmith's shop at Seaham Colliery, 1956. Amongst the onlookers are: Freddy Partridge, Wilf and Johnny Rochester, Billy Henderson, Barrett Murray, Harry Neil, Joe Thompson, Matty Finkel, Tommy Hogg, Roland Withinshaw, Bill Selby, Ronnie Allen and Bonna Northway.

Seaham Colliery High Pit, *c.* 1950. On 11th July 1987, Seaham and Vane Tempest Collieries merged, forming a combined mine with 'a promising future'. In practice Seaham Colliery became redundant and over forthcoming months its fabric was largely dismantled. The High Pit heapstead survived until November 1992, when, without warning, it vanished suddenly from the skyline.

Cutting the first sods of Dawdon Colliery, 26th August 1899. After laying the Foundation Stone at the Docks (see page 60), the party travelled to Dawdon where Theresa, Marchioness of Londonderry and her son, Viscount Castlereagh cut the first sods of the new colliery's two shafts. Lady Londonderry was the first to step forward, naming the colliery 'Dawdon' and the shaft 'Theresa'. The Viscount followed, naming the second shaft 'Castlereagh'. Afterwards, the group posed for a photograph (shown above) before Lord Londonderry and his chief agent, Vincent Corbett, addressed the crowd.

From Dawdon the party travelled to Seaham Hall where lunch was served, followed by an inspection of Seaham Volunteers on the nearby Vicarage Field. In the evening a public fireworks display brought the day to an enjoyable conclusion. The *Seaham Weekly News* reported:

'Messrs Downey, photographers, of South Shields have secured some "Living Photographs" of the Foundation Stone Laying and of Lord and Lady Londonderry and party leaving the grounds of the Sod Cutting, and after his lordship has seen these pictures they hope to have an opportunity of exhibiting them in the town. At the Cycle Church Parade on Sunday they also took a very long and successful picture of the cyclists passing through the park, including portraits of the majority who attended.' Does this unique footage exist today?

Dawdon Colliery during sinking, *c.* 1903. The contract for sinking was originally awarded to Mr Frank Coulson of Durham who commenced at 6 am on 19th March 1900. However, operations were suspended in December 1902 because of flooding and on 20th April 1903, the contract was transferred to the German firm of Gebhart & Koenig who applied newly developed freezing techniques to conquer the problem. After considerable difficulty and several fatal accidents the task was completed on 5th October 1907. Three weeks later, on 23rd October, the first coals, about 25 tons from the Hutton seam, were brought to bank and shipped at the docks aboard the SS *Viscount Castlereagh*.

Dawdon Miners' Institute and adjoining houses for two checkweighmen, Mount Stewart Street, *c.* 1915. The Institute was erected at a cost of £1,600 by Messrs T&E Curry of New Seaham and was opened on 3rd December 1910 by Mr Robert Boad, president of Dawdon Miners' Lodge. After the ceremony a public meeting was held in the Robert Candlish Memorial Hall where a new banner for the Dawdon Lodge was unfurled by Dr F.W. Squair.

Lord and Lady Londonderry photographed with Viscount Castlereagh and mining officials during a visit to Seaham and Dawdon collieries, 6th September 1923. Led by Mr Malcolm Dillon (chief agent), Mr W.A. Swallow (manager of Seaham Colliery) and Mr F. Wilson (manager of Dawdon Colliery), the party inspected the surface and underground workings at both pits and afterwards examined the new houses being built for the Londonderry Collieries Ltd at New Seaham and Dawdon.

Arthur Harman, chauffeur to Mr Frederick Wilson, manager of Dawdon Colliery, *c.* 1925. Mr Wilson took over as manager in September 1919, following the retirement of Mr J. Stanley Cowell who in turn had succeeded Dawdon's first appointed manager Mr E. Seymour Wood in 1904. Mr Wood was in charge for a three year spell during the freezing operations but moved on to take up the manager's post at Murton Colliery in September 1907.

Three pit lads about to start their shift at Dawdon Colliery, date unknown but probably in the 1930s. Boys were employed at the pit from the age of 14, usually starting off at bank on the screens or underground as trapper boys then pony drivers, pulling tubs to and from the loading bays. It was hard work in frightening and dangerous conditions that occasionally proved fatal. The *Seaham Weekly News* reported deaths of two fourteen-year-old driver lads in 1914: Ralph Forster from Longnewton Street, killed at Dawdon Colliery on 18th February and Andrew McKenna of 48 California Street, killed at Seaham Colliery two months later.

Dawdon Colliery St John Ambulance team in the grounds of Vane House, 1950. Helen Street is in the background. On display is a selection of medals and trophies won by the team in recent competitions. Sitting behind the cups in the centre of the front row is Dr Neilan, medical superintendent.

Members of Dawdon Miners' Lodge outside the Miners' Hall, Mount Stewart Street, 17th May 1953. The Hall was built to the design of Councillor J.W. Claxton by Mr P. Duffy on to the rear of the existing Miners' Institute. Seating accommodation was provided for 800 people. As part of the scheme the interior of the Institute was largely reconstructed to improve access and to cater for the increasing demands of the Lodge. Alderman William House, JP, president of the DMA, performed the official opening on 19th December 1914.

Dawdon Colliery Band leading the Lodge Banner along Queen Alexandra Road *en route* to Durham for the 1956 Miners' Gala. Marching at the front is well known Dawdon character Billy Wood with bandmaster and musical director, Stanley MacDonald, following behind.

Dawdon Colliery during reconstruction, *c.* 1959. Before reconstruction, the colliery was worked using manual pillar extraction with steam winders lifting cages loaded with 10 cwt tubs. In 1953 and 1957, modernisation programmes introduced longwall power loading extraction and tower mounted electric

winders. The Theresa shaft (upcast) was re-equipped with two 10 ton skips bringing 450 tons of coal to bank per hour. The Castlereagh shaft (downcast) was re-equipped with two double deck cages, each deck taking one mine car.

Dawdon Colliery from the south, *c.* 1961. Production ended on 26th July 1991 and in the months that followed the haunting sound of hydraulic hammers filled the air as, one-by-one, buildings were turned into rubble. Finally, on 26th January 1992, an emotional crowd gathered in the mist and drizzle to witness seven-year-old Sarah Davie set off charges which sent the Theresa and Castlereagh towers crashing to the ground.

Boring in progress at Vane Tempest Colliery, *c.* 1925.

Plans to sink a third colliery at Seaham were first announced by Lord Londonderry in a speech at the town's Constitutional Club on Thursday 4th January 1923. Work to prepare the site began soon afterwards, one of the first priorities being the laying of railway sidings connecting the colliery with the LNER line near Seaham Hall. As the year drew to a close, Lord Londonderry's son, Lord Castlereagh, cut the first sods of the two shafts on Wednesday 19th December in one of three public engagements marking his coming of age celebrations. The day began with a visit to the Harbour where he was invited to lay the corner stone of a new extension being made to the South Dock. Afterwards, the party travelled to North Road where a number of Aged Miners' Homes were being constructed on a site adjacent to the new colliery. There, Lord Castlereagh also laid a commemorative stone before moving on to the colliery itself where using a silver spade and carved oak wheelbarrow he removed sods from the new 'Vane' (downcast) and 'Tempest' (upcast) shafts. After the ceremony, refreshments were served in the engine house which had been tastefully decorated with chrysanthemums and evergreens. Amidst toasts and speeches, Lord Castlereagh received a gift of two silver decanters, one from the Franco-Belge Co of Brussels, contractors for freezing and sinking and one from the Trefor Boring & Sinking Co of London, contractors for boring.

Construction of the shafts was carried out in three distinct but overlapping stages; boring, freezing and sinking. Work began first on the Tempest shaft, boring starting on 1st October 1924; freezing starting on 18th September 1925 and sinking starting on 16th February 1926. During sinking the frozen limestone was hacked away and drawn to the surface in 2 ton iron kibbles. Progress was interrupted for seven months as a consequence of the 1926 strike but in January 1927 Lord Londonderry proudly displayed the first piece of coal, extracted from a thin 5 inch seam found at a depth of 510 feet. A year later, on 12th January 1928, the bottom of the shaft was reached, 2,116 feet below the surface. Completion of the Vane shaft followed on 18th June.

Londonderry Colliery, Seaham Harbour. 9507

Vane Tempest Colliery approaching completion, *c. 1929*. Celebrations marking the end of sinking were overshadowed by the tragic death of twenty-two-year-old Anthony McCann, a sinker from 2 Benevente Street, who lost his life on 22nd June 1928 whilst preparing a roadway in the Hutton seam. The inquest returned a verdict of 'Accidental Death' and thus McCann went down in history as the colliery's first fatality.

Finishing touches being made to the boilerhouse chimney at Vane Tempest Colliery, *c. 1928*. On 20th June 1929, the first train load of coals, some 230 tons, were despatched to the Docks. Six years in the making and costing over one million pounds to construct, the Londonderry Colliery, more familiar as the Vane Tempest, was finally bearing fruit.

Locals gathered in the playground of Seaham Intermediate School with the Vane Tempest Banner before travelling to Durham for the 1932 Miners' Gala. The image on the banner shows Connishead Priory, the miners' rehabilitation centre, which had opened two years earlier. This was, in fact, the reverse side of the banner. Durham Cathedral was painted on the front, accompanied by the phrase 'Build your Association Firmly and Strong'.

Right: George Whitelock, 1938. On leaving school in 1914, George started work as an apprentice at Dawdon Colliery but two years later left to join the Navy during the First World War. Afterwards he returned to Dawdon and in 1920 moved to Seaham Colliery before finally transferring to Vane Tempest in 1923 when the new pit was being sunk. He was appointed foreman electrician in 1934 and electrical engineer in 1947, a post from which he retired in 1963. A keen local historian, he assembled an interesting collection of old photographs, access to which has kindly been granted for this book.

Workmen in the blacksmiths' shop at Vane Tempest Colliery, 1950. The photograph was taken during a farewell presentation marking the emigration to Australia of blacksmith Ernie Brandt. Ernie is standing in the centre row, fifth from the left with curly hair and open shirt. Kneeling in front, with gleaming white teeth, is youthful looking workmate, Roland Duffell.

Right: The NCB boring tower, photographed by a sea-sick Jim Curry, three miles off the Seaham coast, June 1959. In 1958 the NCB began a seabed drilling programme off the coast between South Shields and Hartlepool to gain a better understanding of reserves in the underlying strata. The boring tower became a prominent part of the coastal scenery, standing 230 feet high, 80 feet across and weighing 700 tons. It was manned by a resident crew of 15.

A coal skip being installed at Vane Tempest Colliery, *c.* 1958. Assisting with manoeuvres are: Paddy Lenox, Tom Wilson, Tom Pausey, Billy Brunning, Frank Smith, Danny O'Connor and Jack Ritchie (in the crane cab).

A rake of tubs passing through No 1 loader at Vane Tempest Colliery, *c.* 1960. Coal production at the pit was suspended on Friday 23rd October 1992. Emotional scenes followed on 4th June 1993 when closure was announced, and in April and May 1994 when the heapsteads were demolished. Today, bleak and empty, the site is poised for redevelopment.

SECTION FOUR

THE DOCKS

A photograph taken at the Docks around 1912 featuring diver Alfred Knapp (left), a mariner from Whitstable who came to Seaham in the late 1890s to work on the South Dock extension. Afterwards he found a permanent post at the Harbour where he worked until his death in 1932. The diver on the right is Daniel Beer.

Laying the foundation stone of the new Docks works, 26th August 1899.

The Harbour and Docks were opened in 1831 by the 3rd Marquess of Londonderry to export coal from his wife's inland pits at Rainton and Pittington. Originally, they were designed to cater for sailing ships of 300-400 tons but by the 1890s these had largely been replaced by steam colliers of over 1,000 tons which could no longer be accommodated. In consequence, trade was lost to Sunderland, prompting the 6th Marquess and his Trustees to seek statutory consent from Parliament to improve and enlarge the Harbour as 'a matter of urgent necessity'. Authority was granted on 12th August 1898 in the form of the Seaham Harbour Dock Act.

The new works were designed by Mr H.H. Wake of Sunderland and carried out under the supervision of Mr W. Molk of Westminster, both acknowledged experts in their field. Messrs S. Pearson & Son of Westminster were appointed contractors, having submitted a fixed price tender of £378,000. The project involved building two new piers, deepening the channel entrance, forming a new deep water dock and providing additional coal shipping facilities. Work began in April 1899, four months before the stone laying ceremony which took place at the site of the new North Pier on 26th August.

Many distinguished guests attended the ceremony which had been arranged as part of Viscount Castlereagh's coming-of-age festivities. Sir Michael Hicks-Beach, Chancellor of the Exchequer and main guest of honour, stepped forward to lay the foundation stone and after addressing the crowd was followed by Viscount Castlereagh who laid a commemorative coping stone. Sir Wheatman Pearson, on behalf of the contractors, then presented the Viscount with a silver model of the pier, which opened as a fine cigar-box. Lord Londonderry concluded the proceedings with a vote of thanks before leading the party to a special train bound for Dawdon Colliery where the second great ceremony of the day took place (see page 48).

The memorable events of 26th August took place in the aftermath of a tragic accident at the old North Pier which claimed the life of seven-year-old Joseph Pickles on Whit Monday, 22nd May 1899. Joseph, who lived at 47 Church Street, had been walking along the pier with three other boys – Frederick Laverick, Joseph Deighton and Nicholas White – when a huge wave swept him into the sea. Laverick was also washed over but Deighton and White escaped and ran to raise the alarm.

Two of the Docks' pilots, Matthew Weirs and Thomas French, hurried to the scene with sailor Samuel Futter, who was working nearby aboard the brig *Sarah Lizzie*. Weirs cast a life-buoy into the sea and succeeded in plucking Laverick from the water. Meanwhile, Futter pulled on another life-buoy, jumped into the waves and grabbed hold of Joseph Pickles. He began swimming towards the pier and was within yards of safety when a huge wave engulfed the pair, dashing them against the wall. Futter lost his grip on the boy but swam out to recover him again only to be dashed against the pier a second time. Tragically, Pickles' jacket split up the back causing the sailor to lose his grasp again and the boy was finally swallowed up in the swell. Desperate, exhausted and himself close to drowning, Futter was pulled reluctantly from the water. The following morning Pickles' body was discovered washed ashore on the south beach, about 80 yards from the sea wall.

At the inquest, held in the Castlereagh Hotel on 24th May, the Coroner, Mr Crofton Maynard, returned a verdict of 'Accidentally Drowned'. In recognition of his gallantry, Samuel Futter was awarded the bronze medal and vellum certificate of the Royal Humane Society. He also received the sum of £10 which had been raised through public subscription as a testimonial to his bravery. The awards were presented several weeks later in a special ceremony at his home town of Wells near Kings Lynn in Norfolk.

Looking out to sea from Lighthouse Cliff over the small block yard and old North Pier, October 1899.

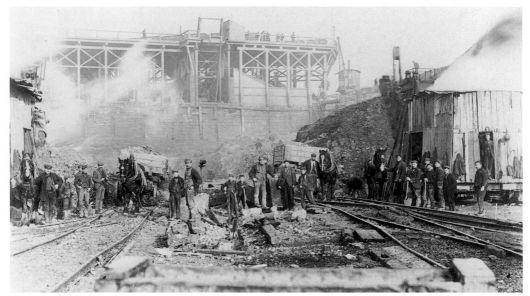

Excavation of the South Dock, *c.* 1902. On the right is an early excavator or steam navvy which was used to fill wagons transporting waste to tipping points at the north of the Harbour. At first the wagons were hauled up the ballast banks but on 5th April 1900 a tunnel connecting the South Dock to the north beach was opened, allowing the equivalent of one day's wagons to pass through in around three hours.

Construction of the new North Pier, August 1903. The piers were built using 20-30 ton blocks of masonry-faced concrete made at the north blockyard near the lime kilns at Lighthouse Cliff. Smaller blocks weighing 4 and 5 tons were used for the inner harbour walls etc. The north pier (1383 feet long) was completed in May 1905 and the south pier (876 feet long) on 25th July 1905. The entrance measured 280 feet.

The SS *Lord Londonderry* at anchor, *c.* 1905. On Sunday 1st August 1903 the *Lord Londonderry*, under Captain John Adamson, became the first vessel to enter the new South Dock after successfully negotiating its temporary entrance. She was also the first to load and leave, setting off at 2 pm on Thursday 6th amid cheers from a large enthusiastic crowd which had assembled on the quayside to witness the event.

The Prime Minister, Mr Arthur J. Balfour, declaring the new Docks open, 11th November 1905. Wind and heavy rain almost ruined the day's programme but a break in the afternoon eventually saw the opening ceremony take place. Afterwards, the Prime Minister left for Seaton Carew whilst the town enjoyed a schedule of festivities, including grand dinners for 200 workers of the Seaham Harbour Dock Co and 300 employees of the contractors, Messrs S. Pearson & Son.

Pit props being unloaded from the collier *Newton* in the North Dock, *c.* 1900. The roof of the old Lifeboat House is visible in the bottom left corner. Cranes serving the quayside were once powered by a steam-driven beam engine which was installed near the North Dock entrance in 1831. It was also used to raise and lower storm booms protecting the gateway, a duty it fulfilled until 1947.

A photograph taken from approximately the same spot showing the North Dock packed with fishing cobles, *c.* 1960. Around 30-40 cobles were based at the Docks at the time, most of which sold their catch 'off the rails' near the entrance to the Harbour. The tradition all but ended in the early 1970s when the entrance was redeveloped and whilst sales continued afterwards on land near Barclays bank, this also ultimately died out.

North Dock, Seaham Harbour

The North Dock, *c.* 1912. On 23rd June 1888 the North Dock was closed for three weeks whilst work to repair and upgrade the facilities was carried out. Large gangs of men, up to 150 per shift, were employed on what was the biggest undertaking at the Harbour since its construction. The Dock was drained and dammed to prevent ingress of water before the gates at the entrance were replaced and rock removed to widen the shipping berths. The programme was completed to schedule on 13th July.

Right: William Miller, *c.* 1919. Mr Miller was born in Seaham Harbour into a family with a rich seafaring heritage. His grandfather, Thomas Ellemore, was one of the first pilots to work at the Harbour and his father, Thomas Miller, had been a pilot there from the age of seventeen. William followed in his father's footsteps. He began his apprenticeship in 1877 and ultimately became one of the best-known seafaring men in the town. For 34 years he was a member of the Seaham Harbour lifeboat and for 24 years served as coxswain, retiring from his duties in 1919. He died at his home, 15 Maureen Terrace, on 22nd April 1926 aged 66.

The *Grappler* at work in the South Dock gateway, 20th July 1920. On 10th November 1919 the gates were torn from their pivots during a tremendous gale, bringing the movement of coal to a standstill. Notices were served on 200 employees and mining at Seaham and Dawdon Collieries was temporarily suspended. Limited trading continued from the North Dock but the South Dock remained closed until April 1921.

Londonderry coal trimmers in the early 1930s. Great rivalry existed between the trimmers of the Londonderry Collieries and those of the South Hetton Coal Co, serving their respective colliers in the South Dock. The South Hetton coals were of superior quality and therefore in greater demand than those of the Londonderry Collieries. Consequently, the South Hetton trimmers were rarely laid idle and generally earned higher wages.

A view of the South Dock in the 1930s featuring three colliers. The one in the centre is the *Hatching* and in the foreground is the *Edenside*. Chauldron wagons are lined up on the staithes and behind, on the skyline, are the redundant Candlish Bottleworks (left) and buildings of the Seaham Foundry Co (right). Between are the old pilots' houses and tenement properties of Pilots' Row.

Workmen at the Docks posing for the camera, *c.* 1947. Left to right are: Joe Reaper, Bill Grant, Jack Hutchinson with George Watson leaning on his shoulders, Les Lee and Sid Wallace. Tragically, Jack and Les lost their lives in separate accidents at the Docks which today are still fresh in the minds of their former workmates.

The Docks football team, 1946-47 season. Left to right, back row: Tommy Taylor, Alfie Ryan, Eddie Tasker, Jack Ridsdale, Jack Fenwick, unknown, Mintie Miller (goalkeeper), unknown, Alan Foots, Vic Oates, Taffy Williams. Front row, Stan Winder, unknown, Jimmy Taylor (with mascot), unknown, unknown, Joe Reaper.

Norman Knapp descending into the water from the divers' punt with Alfie Giles standing nearby in shirt sleeves, *c.* 1950. Norman was probably better known for his role as foreman fitter at the Docks but he also trained as a diver under the guidance of full-time professional Jim Pattison. He was engaged in several assignments during the late 1940s and early 1950s, following in the footsteps of his father, Alfred, who features earlier on page 59.

Workmates larking around in the yard outside the blacksmiths' shop, *c.* 1957. Left to right are: Alan Cooper, Stuart Donaldson, Matty Finkel and Billy Wilson holding the mell. On the block is 'victim' Tommy Johnson. The blacksmiths' shop is the large building behind the crane. Further to the right is the coppersmiths' shop and part of the electricians' shop.

The paddle tug *Seaham* moored in the South Dock, 1957. Built by J.P. Rennoldson & Sons of South Shields, the *Seaham* made her maiden voyage on Monday 24th May 1909 in the company of distinguished officials from Rennoldson's and the Seaham Harbour Dock Company. She was the second tug to have been commissioned from Rennoldson's, the first being the *Lady Helen* which was delivered into port on 18th September 1888 as a replacement for the old tug *Harry Vane*. The *Seaham* served until 1962 when after fifty three years loyal service she made her final trip beyond the piers, to be broken up for scrap.

One of Seaham's blackest days – the Lifeboat *George Elmy* washed up at Dawdon after capsizing in stormy seas on 17th November 1962. The Lifeboat had gone to assist the coble *Economy* and having rescued the five people on board was re-entering the Harbour when it was struck by violent waves and overturned. All five crew and four from the coble were lost. Donald Burrell, the only survivor, died nearly thirty years later. His ashes were cast into the water near the disaster scene on 19th September 1992.

The crew of the replacement lifeboat, *Howard D*, 21st November 1962. Left to right: Capt R. Muir, coxswain; Capt R. Mallam, second coxswain; Mr M. Green, spare hand; Mr J. Findlay, second bowman; Capt R. Hudson, RNLI branch secretary; Mr E. Brown, bowman; Mr A. Farrington, second mechanic; Mr T. Breeds, spare hand and shore helper; Mr T. Turnbull, chief launchman; Mr J. Witten, winchman and spare hand.

SHOPS, PUBS AND FACTORIES

Meek Brothers, Motor Engineers, 9 North Railway Street, *c.* 1925. The Meek brothers started in business as cycle agents in Lord Street, moving to 9 North Railway Street shortly after the First World War. There they established a garage and workshops which around 1930 were sold to William Skillbeck. Other businesses featured in the photograph are James Temple, jeweller Thomas Makay, confectioner and Edgar Snowden, grocer.

The Seaham Harbour Co-operative Society

Staff in the yard of the Castlereagh Road Co-operative store, *c.* 1912

The Co-operative movement in Seaham can be traced to February 1868 when the *Seaham Weekly News* reported that three separate committees, representing 40-50 members from the railway workshops, the Candlish Bottleworks and the chemical works of Watson, Kipling and Co, had been formed to collect the capital required to start trading. Shortly afterwards, the first store, a former grocer's shop occupied by Mr W. Atkinson, was opened in Church Street.

In 1873 the society moved to new, bigger premises in Frances Street, where in 1874 a drapery department was opened, followed by others selling millinery, boots & shoes, hardware, furniture and clothing. In 1875, with sales approaching £12,000, a horse, cart and harness were also introduced.

In April 1884 it was announced that new, extensive premises, costing between £2-3,000 were to be built on a site next to the Castlereagh Hotel. Mr R. Forster was appointed architect and Mr George Douglas of Sunderland, builder. Construction work began in November and was concluded the following year. To commemorate the official opening on 3rd October 1885, a grand tea was held in the lecture hall above the shops, attended by a staggering crowd of around 2,000 people. A meeting and musical entertainment followed in the evening, interspersed with speeches from several distinguished guests, including miners' agent and parliamentary candidate, John Wilson.

The society's first branch store at Stockton Road, New Seaham opened on 26th February 1898. Built by Messrs Lavin Bros from plans drawn by W. & T.R. Milburn of Sunderland, the premises incorporated grocery, butchery and drapery departments, together with stables and accommodation for the manager, Mr J.W. Scott. At the opening, Robert Hunter, one of the founders of the movement in Seaham, addressed the crowd with a history of the society's rapid development before retiring to the nearby Miners' Hall where a meeting, tea and concert brought the day's memorable proceedings to a close.

A second branch was opened in Eden Street, Horden Colliery on 19th May 1905, under the management of Mr R.J. Strangheir, whom for many years had been employed at the Seaham Harbour store. The formal opening took place on 27th May, when around 300 guests from Seaham travelled to Horden along the newly constructed east coast line aboard a special NER excursion train.

The First World War and subsequent economic recession failed to halt investment in new premises. The Horden branch was extended in 1916 and more outlets opened in the 1920s, one of which was on the corner of Lord Street and Frederick Street in Seaham. In 1922 the increasing importance of trade at Horden was formally acknowledged when the business was renamed 'The Seaham and Horden Co-operative Society'. Another change of name followed when a merger with the Station Town Co-operative Society took place on 4th February 1930, marked the birth of 'The Station Town, Seaham and Horden Co-operative Society'. Four years later, on 8th September 1934, a new branch, comprising butchery and grocery departments was opened on the Avenue at Deneside in Seaham.

Changing shopping patterns in the post-war years led to a gradual loss of business and, ultimately, a transfer of engagements to the North-Eastern Co-op in 1970. Meanwhile, several stores had been sold off including those in Lord Street (1968) and Stockton Road (1970). In 1977 the Castlereagh Road store moved its grocery business to the current premises in Green Street and in 1989 transferred its remaining activities to the former Woolworth's store in Church Street. Sadly, the premises in Church Street were to close on 19th June 1993.

Today, the Co-op in Seaham maintains a valuable trading presence whilst its classic former buildings stand as reminders of a bygone age. The New Seaham Branch, re-opened in 1979 as the 'Regency Assembly Rooms', now offers catering and entertainment to a different type of customer. At the time of writing the Castlereagh Road store is awaiting redevelopment which hopefully will preserve the building for many years to come.

Staff outside the New Seaham Co-operative store, *c.* 1935. Left to right: Stan Holley, Mary Alderson, Tom Reay, Nancy Metcalf, Russell Oglesby, Molly O'Connor and William Oglesby.

Staff of the Dawdon branch of the Ryhope & Silksworth Co-op assembled in the yard of the Princess Road store, *c*. 1926. The branch opened in 1911 and rapidly established a strong position, offering consistently higher dividends than those of the Seaham Harbour Society. At its peak some 4,000 customers were on the books but like other stores in the district, it suffered declining sales in the 1950s and 1960s, which finally led to closure around 1969.

Albert Cummins Carter, tailor and milliner, 6 Lord Street, *c*. 1920. Mr Carter came to Seaham around 1890 and worked as a cutter at the Seaham Harbour Co-op before setting up his own business in 1913. He died in November 1930, aged 71 and was succeeded by his son, William. Both are featured in the picture. Mr Carter senior is at the extreme right next to Jane Corkhill,

tailoress. William has a tape measure draped over his shoulders. To his right, wearing the white blouse, is Adeline Smith then Mr Carter's daughter, Sarah.

J.J. Wanless, bakers and confectioners, 23 Church Street, *c.* 1924. A message written on the rear of the photograph reads: 'We had a rush of Bridescake orders during August – 8 for 10 days – here is a postcard showing some of them.' Several employees are missing from the group, including Rebecca Williamson, the author's paternal grandmother. When the photographer called she was on holiday at the popular resort of Billingham!

Roland Mawston Smith, motor engineer, Sunderland Road, New Seaham, 1928. The garage was built in 1928 by John Clark & Son of New Seaham by order of Mr Smith, a former pilot who served with the Royal Naval Air Service during the First World War. Today the premises are more familiar as the Lodge Garage, so-called because they stood in close proximity to the former western lodge house of the Seaham Hall estate.

Metcalfe's staff outside the store at 1 & 2 North Terrace, *c.* 1935. Left to right are: unknown, Jack Alcorn, Sydney Richardson, Mr McCartney, George Chambers, Peggy Wood, unknown, Mr Metcalf, Molly Taylor, Lily Myton, unknown, Danny Brown, Albert Ramsey, Jack Turnbull, unknown, Ted Purvis (manager).

Woolworth's staff on the roof of the Church Street store, *c.* 1947. In fine weather the roof was a popular venue for tea and lunch breaks. Back row: Greta Wright, Ruth Buckley, Joan Robinson, Margaret Allen, Freda Wilkinson, Isa Harris, Audrey Pearson, Lily Heydon, Lily Marwood, Muriel Tiffany, Lotty Johnstone. Middle row: Eleanor Hall, Mrs Henry, Miss Macklam (manageress), Freda Shilling, Evelyn Horn. Front row: Lily Whitwell, Ann Barstow, Dolly Baker, Sheila Traynor, Ivy Johnson, Olive Baron, Edith Rochester.

Doggart's drapers, 58 & 59 Church Street, with blackout boards fitted to the windows, *c.* 1940. At one time there were 14 branches of Doggart's scattered throughout the North-East but eventually all went out of business. The Seaham branch opened around 1923 and closed in January 1981. Today the premises are occupied by Mackay's Ltd.

Sylvia Ballantine (left), Gweneth Goodwin (centre) and Agnes Henderson (right) outside Goodwin's corner shop, 1 Alfred Street East, *c.* 1960. Goodwin's was the busiest of several corner shops in the Ropery Walk area and a favourite of local children who would clamber on to pop boxes to select sweets from the tempting window display. Today the shop is owned by Kernail Singh and is called Ken's Super Store.

The Mill Inn photographed shortly after it was reconstructed by the leasee, Mr Barrett Wells, *c*. 1895. To commemorate the start of rebuilding, family and friends were invited to witness Mrs Wells of the Noah's Ark, North Railway Street, lay the first stone on 5th September 1892. On the occasion, Mrs Wells was presented with a silver mounted trowel by the architect, Mr W. Robson.

The Royal Naval Reserve Arms, 6 Back North Terrace, *c*. 1895. It is not known exactly when this pub first opened but it can be traced in Post Office directories to at least 1886. The license to sell alcohol was revoked on 11th June 1908 and the premises were then used successively as a general dealers,  newsagents and fried fish shop. Like other properties in the area, it was ultimately demolished under a slum clearance order.

The Golden Lion Hotel, 1 South Railway Street, *c.* 1900. The sign above the door refers to Adam Chapman Harrison, who took the lease around 1896. When it expired he bought the premises and adjoining Theatre Royal, remodelling both in a programme which saw the demolition and rebuilding of the old theatre. Mr Harrison held the hotel for over 30 years but on 26th October 1929, at the age of 64, he passed away at his home, Cliff House.

Looking up Back North Railway Street, showing the rear entrance of the Forester's Arms at 10 North Railway Street, 1933. The resident publican at the time was Mr William H. Foster. Dating from at least 1847 and probably from the 1830s, when North Railway Street was constructed, the Forester's stood as one of the town's oldest

pubs for more than a century. It was demolished in 1959 to make way for the enlargement of Snowden and Bailes bakery.

Adam & Eve's Gardens

Dene Cottage Inn, Adam & Eve's Gardens, *c.* 1890.

A visit to any local or national collectors' fair where old postcards are being offered for sale will, in most instances, yield examples featuring Dene Cottage Inn and the surrounding pleasure park known as Adam and Eve's Gardens. The gardens were laid out by Colin Fair on land leased from Lord Londonderry near the mouth of Dawdon Dene and were opened to the public in May 1829. Colin Fair was originally from Norton and had spent several years in Sunderland before moving south with his family to Seaham when the harbour and new town were in the early stages of construction. In 1838, he left Seaham to live in Hawthorn and was succeeded at the gardens by his son, Ralph, who had worked for Seaham brewers Fothergill and Spence, first as a traveller and later as first landlord of the Ship Inn, North Railway Street.

In 1852 the Fairs proudly hosted the town's first flower show, an event organised by the Seaham Harbour Floral, Horticultural and Industrial Society and one which was to become etched indelibly on the town's social calendar. The first show in Adam and Eve's Gardens was followed by others held at different venues including Stafford's Dene, Dawdon Dene and a field which Sebastopol Terrace was later built on. In the late 1850s permission was granted by Lady Frances Anne, Marchioness of Londonderry, for the gathering to take place in the grounds of Seaham Hall. This became the event's permanent home until 1928 when the last show was staged and the organising committee disbanded.

Ralph Fair held the lease until his death on 10th May 1879 at which point it was transferred to his widow, Jane, whose energy had hitherto been directed towards a demanding family of eleven sons and daughters. Jane passed away on 28th November 1894 and was buried alongside her husband in the churchyard at St John's. Her son, Thomas, continued at the Gardens and in

August 1904 saw gardeners from near and far flocking to witness what was then a rare tropical plant – *Yucca-glorisa-suppulosum* – in full bloom. The specimen had been growing in open ground in the Gardens for upwards of 50 years and in the prevailing conditions would have been expected to flower only once in every century. An unusual if short-lived local spectacle.

Around 1908 the tenancy was acquired by Frank Marriott, a cycle dealer with interests in North Railway Street. Marriott later became first landlord of the Red Star Hotel when it opened on 10th June 1932, taking with him the trading license from Adam and Eve's. On his departure the premises were let to Edward Forest who set up a poultry business which a year or so later was taken over by brothers John and Joseph Smith. John was a gardener by trade who had served his time whilst working for Lord Londonderry at Seaham Hall. Their nephew, David Smith, now 75 years of age, went to live with his uncles as a boy following the untimely death of both parents and the Cottage became his home for many years. He can recall fond memories of the time he spent there and the stories of bygone days told by old standards visiting the Gardens as part of their daily routine.

John and Joseph Smith surrendered the lease around 1956, at which point David bought the land, some 3.5 acres, from the Londonderry estate. He went on to develop a thriving market garden, selling eggs and produce direct from the premises and from a mobile shop which toured the streets of Seaham and Dalton-le-Dale. Part of the garden was turned into a boarding kennels for dogs which for almost 20 years were used to impound strays under contract with the local police. Meanwhile, Dene Cottage, which had suffered from years of rot and neglect, gradually became ruinous and in 1965 eventually fell down. In 1989 the deeds were transferred to David's son, also named David, who built a new house in the grounds. He and his family moved in over Christmas 1990 and named their home Adam and Eve's Cottage, ensuring that a familiar name from Seaham's past is carried forward into the new millennium.

A group at the entrance to Dene Cottage Inn, Adam & Eve's Gardens, *c.* 1912.

The Dray Cart Inn, 10 Frances Street, 15th September 1955. The Dray Cart was one of two pubs in Frances Street, the other being the Volunteers' Arms (see facing page). Originally called the Newcastle Dray, the inn was sold to Vaux for £250 on 7th December 1882 and shortly afterwards was renamed the Dray Cart. It survived until about 1960 when it was demolished during a town centre redevelopment scheme.

The yard of the Dray Cart Inn, photographed on the same day as the picture above. Sanitary arrangements are clearly signposted and typical of the period if somewhat rudimentary by today's standards! The overlooking buildings in the background are the houses of Adolphus Street.

Behind the bar of the Castlereagh Hotel in the 1950s. Billy Robinson (right) started his career as a publican in the Lord Byron, moving to the Castlereagh shortly after the Second World War. He later took the Throstles Nest, Shotton, the Alma, Hartlepool and finally, as its first landlord, the Royal Arms, Peterlee. To his right is Chrissie Lacey.

The Volunteers' Arms, 43 Frances Street, 13th June 1956. The photograph shows how the pub once stood in harmony with adjoining houses which, like the Dray Cart referred to earlier, were demolished during the town centre redevelopment scheme. Curiously, the

pub itself was spared and today is still serving customers, standing tall and narrow near the library and St John's Square.

GEO. BOGGON,

PRINTER,

BOOK-BINDER, STATIONER,

AND

GENERAL NEWS-AGENT,

27, NTH. RAILWAY STREET

SEAHAM HARBOUR.

———

DEALER IN PAPER HANGINGS.

A nineteenth century advertisement promoting George Boggon's printing and stationery business at 27 North Railway Street.

Boggon acquired the premises in 1865 and shortly afterwards began publishing the *Seaham Observer*, a weekly newspaper founded in 1858 by local printer David Atkinson. Atkinson was one of at least two printers to emerge in Seaham in the 1850s, the other being John Richardson, founder of the rival *Seaham Weekly News* which entered circulation on 5th May 1860.

The *Seaham Observer* was withdrawn in December 1870 and eight years later Boggon himself went into liquidation. Afterwards he continued working as a journalist from his home at 44 Marlborough Street where he died on 21st October 1904, aged 60. He had established a reputation as one of the best newspaper correspondents in the North of England.

In April 1878, Boggon's business had been sold to William Young, who later took possession of 28 North Railway Street and built-up an extensive printing, stationery and bookbinding enterprise. Following his death, the printing interests were sold to nephew George Young and employee Newton Moorhead. The new partnership of Moorhead and Young traded from premises at 17 Lord Street before relocating to 13 North Terrace in the mid 1930s. In 1946 the business was taken over by J. Greenwood & Sons of South Shields who are still printing there today.

Meanwhile, the *Seaham Weekly News*, based at 3 North Terrace, was enjoying a long and successful print run. Its founder, John Richardson, had died on 29th March 1892 and the following year Stephen Richards became proprietor. Following his death on 21st January 1915, Stephen was succeeded by his son, Edgar Marsh Richards who continued until 1931 when, on 29th September, aged 51, he too passed away. Over the next seven years the paper continued under the management of Mrs Richards but finally, with the Second World War approaching, it was incorporated into the *Durham Chronicle*. News of its sudden demise was reported in the editorial of the last issue, published on Friday, 29th July 1938.

Staff of Willam John Young, printers, 28 North Railway Street, *c.* 1900. Mr
Young is standing on the left. Before coming to Seaham he was employed in
the head office of the Blaydon and District Co-operative Society. He died in
April 1918, aged 70, a victim of the influenza epidemic which swept the
country at the end of the First World War.

Mrs Blanche Lilian Young, widow of the late W.J. Young (above), with her
daughter, Louisa, outside their shop at 28 North Railway Street, *c.* 1920. After
her husband's death, Mrs Young sold the family's printing works and a shop at
20 Church Street but continued trading in books and stationery from North
Railway Street until her retirement in 1925.

Tradesmen at the Londonderry Colliery Workshops, Seaham Harbour, *c.* 1890.
The works were established in 1867 when Earl Vane relocated his colliery
workshops, comprising smiths' shops, carpenters' shops, saw mill and grease
factory, from Chilton Moor to Seaham Harbour. Building began in June, the
new premises being erected adjacent to the engine houses at the Railway
Station. In later years the works evolved into the Wagon Shops.

Work being carried out on a pulley wheel at the Londonderry Wagon Shops,
c. 1918. Far right is George Godfrey Little. As part of the Londonderry Collieries
Group, the works were transferred to the NCB when the coalmines were
nationalised on 1st January 1947. Forty years later, on 20th March 1987, the
shops were closed and six months later were dismantled.

Workmen from Seaham Foundry Co Ltd, *c.* 1908. The foundry was started in 1843 by Robert Wight who sold the business to Messrs Hopper & Radcliffe in December 1870. They withdrew in 1874 and two years later Messrs Cockburn & Sample took over, resuming casting in April 1879 after an extensive rebuilding scheme. In 1899 new owners began trading as the Seaham Foundry Co Ltd, a name the works retained for over 50 years.

The foundry viewed from Ropery Walk in the 1960s. Around 1950 the works was acquired by Sunderland iron founders Jennings Ltd, who continued manufacturing until the late 1960s when the factory finally closed. The site was then redeveloped and today is occupied by warehouses of the Seaham Harbour Dock Co.

Looking north-east from the blastfurnace branch of the Londonderry railway towards the Londonderry Bottleworks, *c*. 1890.

The works was one of two bottle factories to emerge in the early 1850s, the first being the Seaham Harbour Bottle Co, whose managing partner was Robert Fenwick, a Sunderland brewer engaged in bottlemaking on the banks of the Wear at Bishopwearmouth Panns. In 1855 his name became immortalised in Fenwick Row, a terrace of neat tenements erected near the Seaham works. Number 1 was reserved for the Londonderry Hotel, known to locals as 'The Parrot'. One of Seaham's lost pubs, it closed in 1970.

In 1857 the Seaham Bottle Co amalgamated with its rival and neighbour, the Londonderry Bottle Co, which, likewise, was owned by a Sunderland man named John Candlish. In his youth, Candlish had worked as a labourer in Pemberton's Bottleworks at Ayres Quay but left to forge a career in trade and management which brought him back to glassmaking, this time as a partner in the Trimdon Street factory in Sunderland. Then, in 1853, he secured the lease of a site at Seaham from the Marquess of Londonderry and established a factory of his own, naming it the Londonderry Bottle Co in honour of his lordship.

When John Candlish died on 17th March 1874, the works were transferred to brother Robert whom for many years had managed operations at Seaham. Robert was, in turn, succeeded by his son Joseph John Candlish under whose control the limited liability company of Robert Candlish & Son Ltd was formed. In 1913 it became part of the United Glass Bottle Manufacturers Ltd in a move that saw him installed as chairman, but with the First World War approaching, the future for the factory looked uncertain. Ultimately, its fate was sealed by the crippling coal strike of 1921. On 15th April the *Seaham Weekly News* reported: 'In consequence of the shortage of coal caused by the mining dispute, the old established glass bottleworks of Messrs R. Candlish & Son Ltd at Seaham Harbour are closing down. Today's night shift will be the last and after 5 am tomorrow the factory will be idle.' Sadly, it remained so and never re-opened.

The cone of the eighth 'house' falling, with Gallery Row in the background, 1950. At its peak in the late nineteenth and early twentieth centuries, the factory had seven houses in total, a workforce of 600 and the capacity to produce more than 20 million bottles a year. At the time of its closure only three houses were left – the sixth, producing black glass and the seventh and eighth, producing white or non-coloured glass.

Demolition workers engaged in site clearance operations at the Bottleworks, 1950. The demolition contractors, Harbour & General Ltd, began work in 1949 and continued until August 1950 when the last surviving chimneys were felled. A gang from Thompson's of Easington then moved in to level the eight acre site which remained an industrial wasteland until about 1968 when it was landscaped to provide a playing field for Ropery Walk School.

Seaham Harbour Water Works shown before the old pump headgear was dismantled, 14th June 1915. The works were built in 1853 at a cost of £3,700 for the Seaham Waterworks Co but in 1871 were sold to the Sunderland and South Shields Water Co Ltd. They managed the supply for over a century before amalgamating with the Newcastle & Gateshead Water Co Ltd in April 1992.

Right: Seaham Brickworks, *c.* 1964. The brickworks was started in 1868 by Mr J. Daglish, Earl Vane's chief agent, to make profitable use of the waste 'sagger' clay extracted from the Hutton Seam during coal mining at nearby Seaham Colliery. In 1947, following nationalisation of the coal mines, ownership was transferred from the Londonderry Collieries Group to the NCB who maintained output at over five million bricks per year. Firing continued until October 1965 when the factory was eventually closed, almost a century after its foundation.

Seaham & District Laundry, Stockton Road, New Seaham, *c.* 1949. The laundry was established in 1924 by Thompson Dawson who with his brother, Robert, built up a thriving business, employing around 50 staff. In 1949 the firm celebrated its Silver Jubilee but two years later was in mourning, when Thompson died in a car accident near Old Shotton. His son, Robert, then took over and ran the business until its closure in the early 1960s.

Driver Jack Smith at the wheel of one of the Seaham and District Laundry vans, 1925. The vans were once a common sight at Seaham Hall Hospital with whom the laundry had a major contract for cleaning bedding and soft furnishings. They were also regular visitors to the Docks, collecting laundry from ships entering port, to be washed, pressed and returned in preparation for the outgoing journey.

Girls in the machine shop at Barran's clothing factory, Dene House Road, c. 1959. Founded in Leeds in 1851 by Sir John Barran, the company was making garments for over a century before opening up in Seaham in the 1950s. Production began at the Candlish Memorial Hall but transferred to Dene House Road when the factory there opened in 1958. At its peak 420 staff, mainly women, were employed. Today the workforce is 121.

Snowden & Bailes bakery, North Railway Street, c. 1964. The firm developed from a small bakers and grocers store run by brothers Arnott and Edgar Snowden at 6 North Railway Street. In 1928 it became a limited company and later, when John Bailes entered the business, it became Snowden & Bailes Ltd. In 1959 it was extended, taking in numbers 7-18. Snowden's was sold to Baughen's in 1975 and ten years later the factory closed when production transferred to Peterlee. The buildings were demolished in 1994.

SPORT

Swimmers competing at Dawdon 'Pit Pond', 5th July 1952. The 'Pond' was originally a cooling reservoir for Dawdon Colliery but at the end of the Second World War it was converted into a swimming pool for the newly formed Dawdon Colliery Amateur Swimming Club. The club hosted a number of national and international events such as the challenge contest featured in the photograph, between Dawdon and Shotts Swimming Club of Lanarkshire in Scotland.

A regatta in progress, possibly the first, held on 20th July 1873. Densely packed crowds once flocked to this annual event which was struck by tragedy in 1886 when the pilot coble *John & Mary* sank just outside the Harbour with five men on board. Morley Scott, Robert Spoors and William Willis were rescued but Thomas Thurlbeck (23) and Andrew Johnson (33) were drowned. The 26th and final regatta was staged on 6th August 1898.

Left: Thomas Oliver Johnson and his daughter Mary astride a tandem tricycle, *c.* 1896. Cycling was popular in the late 1800s when at least four new clubs sprang up in Seaham Harbour – 'Seaham Harbour' at the Noah's Ark Inn (1888), 'Seaham Harbour Ashmore' at the Bradyll Arms (1893), 'Theresa' at Botcherby's beerhouse, 5 North Terrace (1896) and 'J.J. Candlish' at the Robert Candlish Memorial Hall (1897). The Johnsons lived at New Seaham where the 'New Seaham Londonderry Benevolent Cycling Club', based at the New Seaham Inn (now the Kestrel), had been established since 1882.

Founder members of Seaham Harbour Swimming Club photographed by John Lomax, 1880. Organised swimming in Seaham can be traced to July 1866 when the town's first club was formed at a meeting in the Londonderry Institute. It disbanded in November 1867 but was reformed in August 1880 by the 30 or so enthusiasts featured in the photograph. Far right is James Temple Wightman, who served as swimming master for 28 years.

Ladies from Seaham Harbour Swimming Club gathered near the 'knuckle end', 1930s. In the club's early years ladies were strictly forbidden but were ultimately accepted around 1920. Membership peaked at about 800 in the 1930s but dwindled in the post-war years when alternative facilities opened at Dawdon Colliery and tuition for children was introduced in schools. In 1981 the club was forced to close, a year after celebrating its centenary.

An early team from Seaham Harbour Cricket Club gathered in front of the old wooden pavilion. Although the date is unknown, the surnames of the players have been recorded on the rear of the photograph. Back: McKenna, G.D. Forster, Walker, Gibson, K. Forster, White, Reed. Front: Anderson, Walker, Scorfield, Ferguson, Scott.

George Nelson Francis, *c*. 1930. A native of Barbados, Francis played as a fast right hand bowler for the West Indian Bridgetown Club before signing as 'pro' for Seaham Harbour in August 1928. He made his first appearance in a friendly on 20th April 1929 and entertained the crowds until 1932 when higher wages drew him to Radcliffe in Lancashire.

A late nineteenth century photograph featuring what is thought to be New Seaham 'Ernest' Cricket Club. The club was named after Lord Ernest Stewart (1836-85), youngest son of the 3rd Marquess and can be traced to at least 1873. Matches were played on a field behind Stewart Street at the High Colliery until 1916 when the team finally disbanded. The club had its own banner, the front bearing the words 'Seaham Ernest Cricket Club' and the reverse showing a playing pitch with a bat and ball set next to the stumps.

Seaham Park Cricket Club, Coast League Champions, 1927, 28 & 29. Rear, left to right: Robert Conn, Martin Tempest, Harry Armstrong, Wil Spence, Bill Stephens, John Bryan. Middle: William Spiller, Geoff Harrison, Jas Dent, Mrs Ford, Mr Ford (manager, Seaham Colliery), Joe Wright, Rob Thompson, Dick Weetman. Front row: Matt Adamson, Sam Conn, Frank Armstrong, John Ranson, John Sterling.

Seaham White Star, 1904. Team members, back row, left to right: Miller, Breeze, Chisholm, Williamson, Harris, William Ferguson. Front row: Newby, Bell, Baxter, Jeffery, Hood, Stark, Kelly and Cole. The election poster on the changing hut behind suggests that the photograph was taken in February or March when campaigning for local council elections was in progress. Reference is made to one of the candidates named Johnston Russell Thompson, a builder of 15 Adolphus Street West who was also licensee of the Rose and Crown public house, 13 Church Street. Mr Thompson successfully secured a position on the council that year and retained his seat in 1907 and 1910.

The 'Star' were formed in the mid 1890s and initially were based at the Gasworks Field, a rectangular, grassed area adjoining the southern boundary of Seaham Gasworks. In 1907, the field was acquired for expansion of the factory and the club then moved to the Bungalow Field near Seaham Harbour Cricket Club, where they underlined their status as the town's premier football team. Elected to the Wearside League in 1902-3, they first won the championship in 1904-5, conquering 11 other teams over 22 matches, including arch rivals Seaham Villa and Seaham Albion. The trophy was presented at the Palatine Hotel, Sunderland, on 17th May 1905 and on arriving at Seaham was paraded around the streets to the delight of cheering supporters. A similar scene followed in the 1907-8 season when the club took the title for a second and final time. In 1909 they entered the North Eastern League and in deference to the wishes of the League, changed their name to Seaham Harbour. Many years later a new 'White Star' team emerged, this time at New Seaham, inspired by memories of their legendary predecessors.

Seaham Harbour Cricket Club AFC, *c.* 1921. In early 1923 a proposal was announced to convert the club into a limited company in an effort to bring professional football to the town. Three years later the proposal became reality when on 10th July 1926 the club was registered as the Seaham Harbour Association Football Club Ltd. Unfortunately, the fixtures failed to pull in the crowds and on 15th May 1929 the team was reluctantly wound-up.

Right: John William Miller, right back and captain of Seaham White Star, *c.* 1908. Born in Pilot Row on 18th February 1879, young Billy lost an arm at the age of two in a railway accident just yards from his home. Known affectionately thereafter as 'Stumpy', he was a talented footballer, playing for Seaham Villa in the Wearside League before moving to the 'Star' in 1901. He served several years as captain and collected many prestigious medals during a long and legendary spell in local league football. Known throughout the district, he died on 29th December 1964 at the age of 85.

Seaham Colliery Welfare FC, 1930-31. In 1930 the old Seaham Colliery Recreation team came under the jurisdiction of the local Welfare Committee and was entered into the Wearside League as Seaham Colliery Welfare. A new ground and pavilion costing £3,500 was provided, Viscount Castlereagh performing the opening on 25th October 1930. The team were soon to enjoy early success, topping the League after an impressive first year.

Left: Arthur Lanes with the Wearside League and Seaham Aged Miners' Cups, both won by Seaham Colliery Welfare FC in the 1946-47 season. Arthur was, and still is, a keen sportsman. He played football for several local clubs and cricket for New Seaham Park before qualifying as a referee at the age of 38. An active promoter of sports at both junior and senior level, he currently coaches bowls at the Seaham Park Green.

Seaham United, champions of the Seaham & District League and winners of the Knock-Out Cup, 1948-49. The photograph was taken in the yard of the Dawdon Hotel and shows Mr Ryles, proprietor of the Princess Road ice cream parlour, presenting the trophies. Looking on is mascot Billy Robinson.

Football supporters from Seaham photographed outside their sea-front hotel during a weekend trip to Blackpool, 15th January 1949. The fans had travelled to watch Sunderland play Blackpool in a league match which attracted a crowd of 25,000. The game was drawn 3-3, Sunderland goals being scored by J. Robinson, T. Reynolds and the legendary Len Shackleton.

Members of Seaham and District Motor Club, *c.* 1929. Motor engineer Roland Mawston Smith, standing third from the right wearing a dark cap and light mackintosh, was one of the club's leading lights. Two other members who may or may not be present in the photograph are Randolph Mather and Matty Hunter, owner of the Church Street Billiard Hall.

Seaham CW Bowls Team, winners of the District Welfare Cup, 1938. The green at New Seaham was laid out at a cost of £350 by Messrs Kent and Brydon of Darlington on land given by the Marquess of Londonderry. Councillor T. Brough, manager of Seaham Colliery, performed the opening on 19th August 1905 before the inaugural match between teams from Seaham and Mowbray Park, Sunderland. The result was a draw 79-79.

Dawdon Welfare Ladies Bowls Team, April 1954. Back row, left to right: Martha Robson, unknown, Mrs Dobinson, Kate Reynolds (vice chair), Olive Tarn, Elsie Thompson, Elsie Brammer, Mrs Burnett, Isa Hathaway. Front row: unknown, Barbara Renton (treasurer), Mrs Gibson (secretary), Mary Leighton (assistant secretary), Mrs E.A. Anderson (president), Ivy Green, Elsie Miller (chair). The team was formed on 16th September 1953.

Four members of Seaham Sea Angling Club posing on the south pier in the 1950s. The club was formed in July 1912 and held its first meetings in the Robert Candlish Memorial Hall on the first Thursday in every month. The 6th Marquess served as president and Mr Walter Coates as

secretary. Today, members meet in their own premises, Clifford House, named after the club's president, David Clifford. It was opened on 18th March 1984.

The King's Arms Darts Team, *c*.1938. Seaham and District Darts League was formed in October 1936 and initially comprised 16 teams enrolled from Dawdon, Seaham Harbour, New Seaham and Ryhope. The Queen's Head Inn, Ryhope, claimed the League Winners Cup in the inaugural season and were presented with the trophy by its donor, Mrs J. Hudson, on 8th September 1937 at a gathering in Seaham RAOB Club.

Staff from Snowden & Bailes outside the North Railway Street factory with trophies won in tug-of-war and five-mile-walk contests at the annual sports meeting at Scarborough, *c.* 1965. Left to right are: Dora Banks, Anne Willis, Jack Reekie, Pat Banks, Hilda Carver, Nancy Williamson, Marie Bamborough, Clive Smith, Eileen Appleby, Dorothy Banks, Jenny Graham, Jimmy Plane.

CHURCH AND CHAPEL

Members of the congregation gathered in front of the Independent Methodist Church in Enfield Road, New Seaham during the jubilee celebrations, 26th March 1927. The church was constructed in 1886 and was dedicated during a special service held on 14th December. So numerous were the visitors that five sittings had to be organised at the public tea that followed afterwards. In 1977 the church celebrated one hundred years of worship at New Seaham where it still holds services today.

st Mary's   old Seaham

The Anglo-Saxon Church of St Mary's, Seaham Village, 1908. Described by Pevsner, in his guide to the Buildings of England, as one of the most worthwhile of the small churches in the county, St Mary's stands perched on the clifftops about a mile to the north of the town.

In March 1997, an excavation of the cemetery, lying partly within the garden of nearby Seaham Lodge, revealed the presence of at least six human skeletons which were carbon-dated to between AD 660 and AD 880. County Archaeologist, Niall Hammond, concluded: 'It makes the site possibly older than Jarrow and Monkwearmouth and places Seaham as one of the earliest Anglo-Saxon Christian sites in England.'

The church has many interesting and unusual features, from Anglo-Saxon windows in the nave to a course of herringbone masonry in the north wall and a sundial on the porch dating from 1773. More can be found inside, such as a nail headed piscina and aumbry, a Jacobean font, an Elizabethan pulpit and Georgian high box pews. A visit is, therefore, recommended but take time to explore the old memorials in the churchyard, some of which were the work of local resident 'Jacky Brough'. His carvings can be distinguished by a tasteful flourish given to the capital letters and the *Aet* (aetas) and *Obt* (obit) for 'aged' and 'died'.

On the south side of the church and a little to the west of the porch are three table tombstones whose inscriptions are barely legible if at all. The most southerly is that of Frances Pailethorpe, butler to Ralph Milbanke of Seaham Hall, who died whilst returning from Sunderland on the evening of 31st October 1769. The middle stone is that of Captain George Williams, buried 1785. The northernmost, which is raised and bears a Latin inscription, is to the memory of William Martin, yeoman, who was interred on 16th November 1698. Two stone posts, about two feet high and rudely dressed, once stood at the foot of this tomb and were said to have been the remains of the ancient village cross. Today, they are nowhere to be seen.

The tombstone of Thomas Todd, which stood in the churchyard at St Mary's, on the south side of the pathway leading up to the porch. It was once commonly believed that the skull and crossbones carving signified the site of a pirate's grave but in fact such carvings were relatively common and typical of the period. In the 1970s, the stone was brought inside the church by Revd Roy Brain and today rests near the font, beneath the Baptistry window.

Right: Revd Angus Bethune JP, c. 1905. Born on 8th March 1811, Angus Bethune was the eldest son of Revd Hector Bethune of Alness. His entire clerical career, dating from 1841, was spent in the Diocese of Durham, first as curate of St Hilda's, South Shields (1841-45) then as first vicar of Seaham Harbour (1845-59) and finally as vicar of (Old) Seaham, from 1859 until his death in 1908. A prominent social figure, he served on several local committees and in 1846 became Seaham Harbour's first Justice of the Peace. He died at Seaham Vicarage on 24th May 1908, aged 97 and was buried in the churchyard at St Mary's.

St John's, Blandford Place, with the incumbent vicar, Revd James Colling inset, *c*. 1923. St John's was opened on 7th June 1840 and became the Parish Church of Seaham Harbour when the parish was created on 23rd August 1843. In 1885-6, during the period of Revd Colling (1874-1923), a new chancel was added, increasing the number of sittings to 650. Inside, are several interesting memorials dedicated to members of the Londonderry family.

Right: An interior view of St John's, showing the chancel and east window in the 1920s. The window was blown out during the Second World War but later renewed during restoration work carried out in 1952. To the left of the window are two of four large panels commemorating the four Northern Saints that were also destined for restoration but after failed attempts they were eventually painted out. Suspended from the ceiling are the old gas mantles, removed when the church was electrified. The new electric installation was dedicated by the Revd Ralph Watson, Rural Dean of Houghton-le-Spring on Sunday, 18th August 1935.

St John's Church Council, 1928. Standing, left to right: R. Bainbridge, W. Nicholson, W.S. Anderson, R. Anderson, Revd C.R. Appleton, unknown, M. Dillon, R. Barkess, J. Brown, W.B. Cockburn, J.M. Pollock, T. Dobson, W. Scott. Centre: Mrs Appleton, Mrs Snaith, Mrs Pollock. Front: J.W. Scott, T.S. Scorfield, Miss Scott, Miss Stoddard, Miss Clegg, Mrs J. Brown, Mrs G.S. Boggon, Miss S. Boggon, Mrs W.B. Cockburn, H. Dobson, R. Wilson.

Right: A photograph of the eight bells and brass commemorative tablet installed in St John's to mark the centenary of Seaham Harbour, November 1929. The bells were cast by Messrs Gillett and Johnson of Croydon and weighed from nearly half a ton (tenor) to two hundredweights (treble). Operated by a clavier on the same principle as a piano keyboard, the chime was designed to be played by only one person. Bishop Henson performed the dedication ceremony during evensong on Sunday, 1st December 1929 at the invitation of the vicar, Revd Charles Appleton and in the presence of Lord and Lady Londonderry.

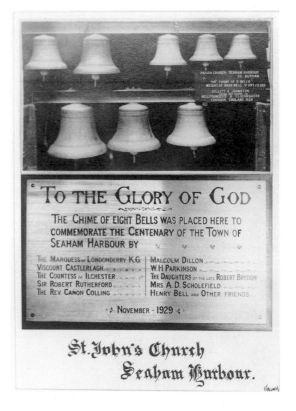

The Cemetery, Princess Road, Dawdon, 1927. Constructed by Mr Ralph Sanderson of Durham to the designs of Mr W. Foster, the cemetery cost £3,400 to complete. Almost half (£1,650) was consumed by the superintendent's house and two chapels. The chapel in the photograph, featuring its original spire, served members of the Church of England and was consecrated by Bishop Lightfoot on 27th September 1885. The other chapel, out of picture to the left, served non-conformists.

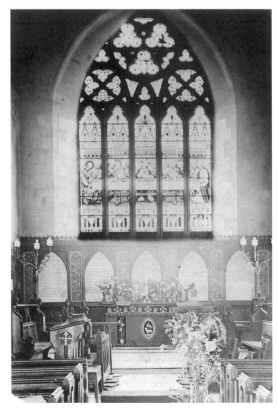

Right: The Chancel, Christ Church, New Seaham, *c.* 1900. Built in 1855-60 by Lady Frances Anne in memory of her late husband, the 3rd Marquess, the church was consecrated on 21st November 1860. The photograph shows the chancel east window, portraying a scene from 'The Last Supper', beneath which are five inscribed tablets. Today these are no longer visible, though possibly still in existence, concealed behind a carved oak reredos that now decorates the wall. Erected by parishioners as a memorial to the 6th Marquess, the reredos was unveiled by the Marquess of Zetland on 18th December 1915.

Joseph Birkbeck, *c.* 1900. Mr Birkbeck was born in 1839 and spent his early years at Pittington, working at the colliery from the tender age of ten. In 1867 he came to work at Seaham Colliery and was appointed organist, choirmaster, clerk and verger at Christ Church. After leaving the pit in 1881, he became postmaster for New Seaham, a position he held for 30 years. He served the church as organist and choirmaster for 50 years, retiring from both positions in 1917, but continued as clerk and verger until shortly before his death. In 1929, on his 90th birthday, parishioners and friends celebrated his memorable career which had witnessed 7,113 baptisms, 1,885 marriages and 5,317 burials. Three years later, on 5th January 1933 he died at home, aged 93. He had been parish clerk for 65 years.

Seaham Harbour Salvation Army Band photographed in 1919 during the Army's Jubilee celebrations. The jubilee coincided with the 42nd anniversary of the organisation's arrival in Seaham Harbour. During the celebrations a musical festival was held on the evening of 16th August in the United Methodist Church, involving around 130 instrumentalists and 60 songsters from the Sunderland, Monkwearmouth, Murton and Seaham Harbour bands.

The 'old' Catholic Church of St Mary Magdelene, Londonderry Road, *c.* 1905. Opened in 1870 during the ministry of Revd Father Green, the church was also used as a school before the schools in Vane Terrace were built. In 1907 it was succeeded by a new, bigger church, built a few hundred yards further west on a site bought from the Marquess for £500. The old church was then handed over to the schools but was ultimately demolished around 1975.

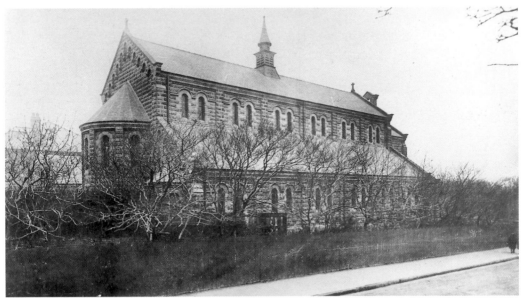

The 'new' Catholic Church, of St Mary Magdelene, Londonderry Road, *c.* 1913. Built in the Romanesque style using bricks of moulded concrete, the church was designed to hold a congregation of 500. The architect was Mr Thomas Axtell of Ryhope, whose work included the churches of St Joseph, Millfield, and St Patrick, Ryhope. Construction began in July 1907 and ended several weeks later, the formal opening taking place on 19th September.

United Methodist Free Church, Church Street, 1905. In 1839 the United Methodists bought two neighbouring cottages in Church Street and converted the upstairs into a church which became known locally as the 'Tabernacle'. A new church and Sunday School were built in 1866 and rebuilt in 1877, incorporating an adjoining cottage to the west. Fire broke out on Sunday, 20th March 1904 reducing the building to a shell but within weeks rebuilding was underway. The new church opened on 29th July 1905 and remained in use until 18th February 1969 when the congregation held their final service before moving to the Wesley Church in Tempest Place. Eventually the building was demolished to make way for a new Boots store which is still in business there today.

1st Seaham Boys Brigade outside the United Methodist Free Church, Church Street, 1937. The brigade was established in Seaham in the late 1880s but disbanded before the First World War. In July 1937, they were reformed at the Methodist Free Church, under Revd Merson Birnie, chaplain (third left, second row), Mr W.N. Moorhead, secretary and treasurer (fifth left, second row) and Mr T. Dixon, captain (fourth left, second row).

Members of the Dawdon 'Ever Welcome' lodge of the Independent Order of Good Templars gathered to celebrate the opening of their new meeting hall in Strangford Road, 11th December 1937. Around 150 people witnessed Mr Bruce Gordon of Tynemouth, the Northumberland District Chief Templar, perform the official opening. The ceremony was followed by a presentation of gifts and a recital given by the Hope of Silksworth Lodge Choir.

Right: A cake made for the 21st birthday of St Hild & St Helen's, Dawdon, 1933. The celebrations began on Friday, 10th February with a sermon by Revd E.W. Bolland, the first vicar of Dawdon and incumbent vicar of Pittington. A social gathering followed in Dawdon Parish Hall, where Mrs Bolland was invited to cut the first tier of the cake and Mrs Duncan, wife of the vicar, Revd James Duncan, the second. Amongst the guests were Mr Edward Gustard, the first baby baptised in the church and Mr and Mrs A.J. Lowther, the first couple to be married. The third tier was cut on Saturday 18th by Lady Londonderry who opened a sale of work in aid of the church.

The interior of All Saints' Mission, Deneside, *c.* 1934. Catering for the spiritual needs of the newly constructed Carr House Estate, the mission was built in asbestos at a cost of £950 by the Alnwick Construction and Engineering Co. The land, amounting to about an acre, was given free by Lord Londonderry. It was opened by Mr Malcolm Dillon on All Saints' Day (1st November), 1932 and dedicated by Herbert Hensley Henson, Bishop of Durham.

Ada Nelson, the oldest member of All Saints' Mission, cutting a cake at the Silver Jubilee party in 1957. Standing to her left is Revd Norman Maddison who succeeded Revd Oswald Noel Gwilliam as vicar in September, 1948. The mission was demolished to make way for All Saints' Church which was erected at a cost of £15,000 by local builder Jack Tomlin to the designs of local architect Harry Dobson. It was opened by Bishop Harland on 20th June 1965.

Derek Ellwood, captain of New Seaham 'Jubilee' Methodist's football team, being presented with the All England Methodist Cup, April 1950. On their way to success the team produced a string of memorable performances, beating Manchester (5-3), Leeds (5-3) and Sheffield in the semi-finals (5-1). In the final, held on 15th April at York City's ground, Seaham hammered Luton 7-0. Under a different line-up the Jubilee won the cup again the following season, earning themselves a legendary place in Seaham's footballing history.

Choristers from St John's on the staircase at Seaham Hall Hospital in the mid 1950s. The choir were regular visitors to the hospital, especially on Christmas Eve, when, during a tour of the wards, hymns were sung to the sick and convalescing, accompanied by Billy Spoors on the portable pedal organ.

IN UNIFORM

Eliza Adams (née Walker) and husband, John Benson, *c.* 1916. During the First World War, Mrs Adams served as a voluntary nurse at the Mission House Hospital whilst her husband fought as one of the 5,000 or so men enlisted from Seaham Harbour, Dawdon and New Seaham. Fortunately, both survived their experiences. After the war, Mr Adams returned to his job as a pattern maker at Seaham Colliery and later helped construct the casework for the War Memorial Organ at Christ Church.

Major F.J. McKenzie with the team of Seaham Volunteers that took first prize at the annual Scottish Artillery convention at Barry Links, July 1898. Over 200 men from Seaham took part in the event that year, departing by special train on 20th July. Officers accompanying Major McKenzie were Major Bernard, Captain Dawson, Lieutenant Warham, Lieutenant A.C. Thompson, Lieutenant Allison and Captain & Adjutant Johnston, R.A.

Left: Sergeant John Holland in the uniform of the Seaham (2nd Durham) Artillery Volunteers, *c.* 1895. The Brigade were formed at Seaham Harbour in 1860 and initially comprised two batteries, rising rapidly to twelve as membership swelled and additional detachments were formed at New Seaham, Rainton, Old Durham and Silksworth. Over 1,000 strong, the unit became one of the largest volunteer corps in the United Kingdom and won many prizes in artillery competitions at Shoeburyness and Barry Links. In 1908 it was incorporated into the newly formed Territorial Army and renamed the 3rd Northumberland Field Artillery Brigade.

Members of the Londonderry's Own Boy Scouts about to depart on their journey to the International Scouts' rally at Copenhagen, Denmark, Wednesday 2nd July 1913. Of twenty-four British Scouts attending the rally, sixteen were drawn from the Seaham Harbour Troop: J. Drennan, J. Nash, S. Hunter, E. Wallace, I. Armstrong, R. Puncheon, R. Thompson, A. Redshaw, A.C. Harrison, R. Mackey, A. Hood, C. Flack, R. Anderson, Chas Fairburn, A. Forster and instructor C.W. Spanton. In charge was District Scoutmaster, Lieutenant T.J. Abbott of Seaham Harbour whom, on this occasion, was also responsible for the entire British Troop.

Lieutenant Abbott, accompanied by twelve of the boys, left Seaham aboard the Londonderry steamer *Seaham Harbour* shortly after 2 pm. The remaining three, accompanied by Instructor Spanton, left Sunderland aboard the Danish steamer *Randelesborg* early the following morning. Lord Londonderry's chief agent, Mr Malcolm Dillon, and Mr D.N. Grimes subsidised the fare, which for the other British Scouts was £3 15s return from Hull to Copenhagen. However, members of the Seaham Troop paid only £1.

The party landed on Saturday 4th July after a rough passage, most of the boys suffering violently from sea-sickness. After a short spell in Copenhagen they were transferred by passenger steamer to Aarhuus and from there to Kalo Castle in Jutland where they were met by some 500 Scouts from Denmark and others from Germany, Switzerland, Russia, Spain Italy, Belgium, Holland, Norway and Sweden.

During their stay the boys took part in numerous activities including a sham war fought between 'Turkish' and 'Bulgarian' armies, each comprising around 300 Scouts. Lieutenant Abbott led the Turks to victory and was presented with a medal in recognition of his skilful manoeuvres. Several activities featuring the British Troop were captured on 'cinema film' including parades and inspections attended by members of the Danish Royal Family.

On the evening of 18th July the boys took part in a grand parade marking the end of the rally before returning to Copenhagen and finally to Seaham where friends and family were waiting to welcome the boys home and hear stories of their great adventure.

Lady Londonderry with the Seaham and Hawthorn Girl Guides, 2nd October 1913. The photograph was taken to commemorate the opening of the new Guides' HQ in the garden of Dene House, home of Norah Dillon, the Seaham Troop captain. Miss Dillon is standing immediately left of Lady Londonderry. To the right is Nira Penelope Pemberton, daughter of Richard Laurence Pemberton of Hawthorn Tower and captain of the Hawthorn Troop.

Left: A typical portrait photograph from the Sunderland studio of Clem Humphries featuring three well presented Sea Scouts, 1920. Standing in the centre wearing a leather glove on his right hand is Tom Cooper. The glove concealed injuries he had sustained in a recent accident at Dawdon Colliery, including the loss of his thumb and little finger. Sitting on the left is J. Robson and on the right H. Bamborough.

Three young soldiers from the First World War. Seated right is Private Billy Nelson who enlisted at the age of seventeen with the 14th Battalion DLI a month after war was declared. His father had been taken prisoner in Germany at the outbreak of war aboard the collier *Seaham Harbour* and shortly after signing up he lost his mother, leaving him responsible for his sister Norah, aged 13, and brother Harry, aged 10. Having endured some of the bloodiest horrors of the conflict whilst fighting at Ypres, young Billy went absent without leave on the anniversary of his mother's death and again went missing two months later. Deeply disturbed and clearly in need of help he was instead court marshalled, field punished and sentenced to death. He was shot on the Somme at 5.15 am on 11th August 1916.

Staff and patients outside New Seaham Mission House Hospital, *c.* 1916. Mission House was formerly the Seaham Colliery Manager's residence which stood next to the High Colliery Schools. During the First World War it was made available to the military for use as a War Hospital, together with Seaham Hall, Vane House and Seaham Infirmary. The Hospital dealt with 650 patients, Mrs W.A. Swallow, the Colliery Manager's wife, serving as Commandant.

The crew of the German collier *Comet* being marched up Church Street shortly after the outbreak of the First World War, 11th August 1914. As soon as war was declared, Customs Officials proceeded to the Harbour where the *Comet* was berthed and arrested the crew as prisoners-of-war. On 11th August they were handed over to the military who escorted them, via Church Street, to the station where they left by the 5.20 train for Sunderland.

The crew of the Londonderry collier *Seaham Harbour* photographed in a German prison camp, 1916. At the outbreak of war the ship was *en route* to Hamburg under the command of Captain Thomas Shilling but on arrival she was intercepted by the German Navy and her crew detained as prisoners-of-war. Captain Shilling later became ill and was eventually repatriated but the rest were held in Germany for the duration of the war.

Seaham Girl Guides on parade in the grounds of Dene House during rehearsals for the town's forthcoming Peace Celebrations, May 1919. The Celebrations took place on Saturday 19th July 1919, starting at 10.30 am with a procession of military and social organisations and ending at 10.30 pm with a bonfire on the seabanks in North Road. In the afternoon and evening, musical programmes were played on the Terrace Green by Dawdon Colliery Band.

Right: The front page of a Souvenir Programme printed to commemorate the Seaham Harbour Peace Celebrations. Because Peace Celebration Day took place in the school holidays, it was decided to postpone the school children's entertainment until the first week of September when the scholars were entertained to tea and sports at the Jubilee Grounds. The programme was as follows: Monday 1st September, Seaham Harbour C of E and Central Council Infants; Tuesday 2nd, Dawdon Council; Wednesday 3rd, Upper Standard, Princess Road; Thursday 4th, Roman Catholic and Friday 5th, Seaham Harbour Council.

Go to T. FALLOWFIELD for all your Clock and Watch Repairs.

PEACE SOUVENIR
and
PROGRAMME OF FESTIVITIES
1919

HOSTILITIES COMMENCED AUG. 4, 1914

ARMISTICE SIGNED NOV. 11, 1918

H.M. King George V.

Containing

Programme of Seaham Harbour Peace Celebrations,
JULY 19th, 1919,
AND
Concise History of the Great War.

PRICE, THREEPENCE.

Published by MOORHEAD & YOUNG, Printers, Lord Street, Seaham Harbour.

Lord Londonderry inspecting members of the newly formed 1338 (Seaham) Squadron Air Training Corps, April 1941. Lord Londonderry was an active national promoter of the Air Defence Cadet Corps movement and was president of the Seaham Squadron which was formed on 1st April 1941. Flight Lieutenant John C. Jennings, Seaham's first Commanding Officer, is shown standing left of Lord Londonderry wearing spectacles and dark suit.

Home Guards outside the Drill Hall, Castlereagh Road, *c.* 1941. Included in the group are, back row: Billy Hutchinson (third left). Middle row: Ridley Black (fourth left), George Whitelock (fourth right), Eric Armbrister (second right). Front row: Mavis Black (extreme left), Commanding Officer, Colonel Richard Laurence Stapylton Pemberton (fifth left), Billy Clifford, (third right) and Betty Thompson (extreme right).

Seaham Auxiliary Fire Brigade outside No 1 station in Foundry Road, *c.* 1941. The station in Foundry Road, in charge of J.B. Proud, was one of three fire stations serving the district in the Second World War. The other two were located at the former Infectious Diseases Hospital in Princess Road, under W.E. Purdy and at Bank Head Street, under S.O. Stephenson.

Right: A moment of light relief during the dark days of the Second World War. The photograph was taken outside Deneside Air Raid Warden's headquarters, located in the Council Yard near the bottom of the Avenue. In the centre, sporting a First World War German helmet and apparently impersonating Adolf Hitler, is George Goodridge who lived up the road at 33 Hexam Avenue. The identity of his captors in the gas masks has yet to be revealed!

Wardens Services, Group C, May 1942. In the Second World War, Seaham was the hardest hit district in Durham County in terms of casualties and damage to property. Nine 'major' air raids were experienced between August 1940 and May 1943, resulting in the loss of 52 lives and 224 injuries. A church, a pub and 157 houses were also destroyed in direct hits, though many more properties were damaged and ultimately had to be demolished.

Flight Sergeant Leslie Hood, September 1944. Leslie joined the RAF in 1941 at the age of seventeen and ultimately served as a navigator in 582 (Pathfinder) Squadron. In the early hours of 29th June 1944, whilst carrying markers destined for the railway marshalling yards at Blainville-sur-l'eau, near Nancy, France, his Lancaster was shot down, killing three of the seven crew on board. Leslie bailed out and was helped by the local Resistance who provided refuge at various safe houses until he was liberated during the American advance on Paris. He returned to Seaham in September 1944, just in time to celebrate his 21st birthday with beloved wife, Olive, his bride of only six months.

5th Seaham (Christ Church) Scouts Band outside Mission House, New Seaham, *c*. 1947. The band was formed in 1933 and held their first public parade in April the following year. Sitting at the front behind the drum, holding a baton and cornet, is bandmaster James Barstead who was also secretary and choirmaster of the Salvation Army Senior Band. To his right is Scout Master Fred Venner and to his left Revd Hogg, vicar of Christ Church.

Right: Norman Bluett, 1955. Norman began work at Dawdon Colliery in 1925 at the age of 15 but left in 1928 to join the Merchant Navy. Two years later he returned to Dawdon where he worked until his retirement in 1974. In 1935 he joined the St John Ambulance Brigade class at the colliery and in 1948 joined the uniformed brigade, becoming a founder member of the Dawdon Colliery Division. His services to the brigade were recognised in 1960 when he was made a Serving Brother and again in 1990 when he was promoted to Serving Officer. A familiar local figure known to many, he died on 4th February 1992 aged 82.

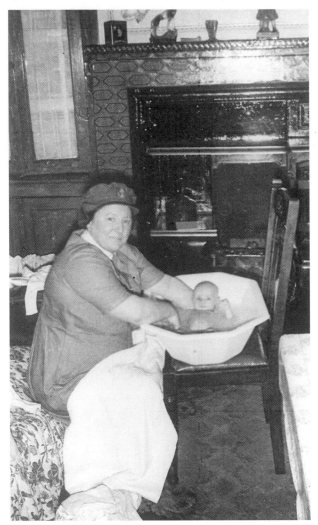

Well known Seaham midwife, Elsie May Bluett (Norman Bluett's sister), bathing one of her 2,529 deliveries around 1950. Miss Bluett took up nursing in 1929 and after training for a year in London at the famous Annie McCall Midwifery College, returned to practice in Seaham. Four years later she moved to Stanley but in 1937 came back to Seaham when Durham County Council assumed responsibility for the service. She retired on her 60th birthday, 25th May 1967, having served 38 years in midwifery, 30 of which were spent in Seaham. After a long and happy retirement she finally passed away on 15th August 1992 at the age of 85.

Help Preserve Our Images Of The Past

Do you have photographs of Seaham or neighbouring communities such as Murton, Hawthorn, Easington etc showing scenes similar to those published in this book? If so, and you would be willing to loan them briefly for copying and possible inclusion in a future volume, please contact the author, Trevor Williamson, on (0191) 5270646.